The
Da Vinci
Curse

Life design for people with
***too many** interests and talents*

CREDITS

Many of the pictures used in this book come from flickr.com. Credit is given for each, which are here reproduced with the permission of the rights holders.

Picture in the cover: Jonas Bergsten (Creative Commons).

All graphics by the author.

At the moment this book was finished the author has no affiliation with any of the companies or brands mentioned in this book.

COPYRIGHT

The author has endeavored to provide information about the copyright status of the content and to identify any other terms and conditions that may apply (such as trademarks, rights of privacy or publicity, donor restrictions, etc.); however, the author can offer no guarantee or assurance that all pertinent information is provided or that the information is correct in each circumstance. It is your responsibility to determine what permission(s) you need in order to use the content and, if necessary, to obtain such permission.

The ideas in this book are either original, or come from notes I scribbled well before I had any intention to publish them; that is the reason why some source citations might be missing. I simply no longer remember where I took those ideas from. If you are, or know, the author or rights holder of any content in this book, please write an email and I will gladly include the source in future editions; the same is valid for comments and interesting information. The transcripts of the movies are included as humorous or cultural references; the copyright belongs to the corresponding rights holders. Any comments regarding prescription drugs are not to be taken as recommendations, only as a personal opinion from the author, who is not a medical professional. In case of any question refer to a qualified physician.

© 2012 by Leo Lospennato. All rights reserved. No part of this book covered by copyrights hereon may be reproduced or copied without written permission, except for brief quotations embodied in articles and reviews, citing the source.

ISBN 978-1523244874

First edition, October 2012

Please address all requests to hello@daVincicurse.com

Visit the book's website: www.daVinciCurse.com

About the author

(Text and photo: Gardenia Fair)

Being baptized "Leonardo" proved to be a cursing omen: Touched by a Renaissance spirit, Leo is a computer engineer, a guitar maker, a judo blue belt, a lover of mathematics, a magazine editor, a polyglot, and a journalist. If he could, he would also be an astronomer and a rock star and would pursue a Nobel Prize in something cool.

Truth be told, that "Renaissance spirit" also manifests in the form of the shameless affair he maintains with Italian cuisine—a mix of heritage and hobby.

But from time to time Leo also tests his luck in a yet more inspiring activity: sharing his thoughts and experiences in the form of a book.

Born in Buenos Aires in '68, Leo now lives in Berlin, Germany, with his wife Andrea and Tango, their black miniature schnauzer.

Dedication

To my mom, Marta:
harbinger of apocalyptic asteroids,
scourge of all sorts of chocolates,
being of light,
bearer of joy.

Thanks to:

Baltazar Avendaño, Mariusz Czepczyński, Daniel Areal, and **Tita Kaisari-Ernst** for their generous and invaluable comments on the draft of this book.

My family and friends, for being there.

My wife, **Andrea,** for her love, support, and generation of ideas.

Contents

Welcome, foxes 6
(Very short) introduction 8

PART I
1 - The Da Vinci Curse: Signs, Causes, Dangers 12
2 - The Age Of Specialization: Living In A Vertical World 24
3 - The Answer To Life, The Universe And Everything 30
4 - Typical DVC: Avoidance, Inconstancy, Blockages 38
5 - The Shadow: Cups And Cakes With Our Dark Side 46
6 - Individuation: To Be Or Not To Be (You) 59
7 - Rites Of Passage: Stepping Into A New World 67

PART II
8 - Inventory Of Dreams 78
9 - Wishes vs. Talents vs. Money 94
10 - Work Styles, Work Areas, Work Roles 104
11 - Life Balance: Maslow's Pyramid, With A Twist 115
12 - Your Portfolio Of Activities: Cows, Dogs, And Stars 120
13 - Pendings: Just Business 126

PART III
14 - Obstacles And Traps 134
15 - A small catalog of overrated things 146

Farewell 152

Welcome, foxes

> *Most people believe we have free will. That we all choose our path. Sometimes the path is clear... sometimes not so much. Every twist, every turn can challenge our sense of direction.*
>
> *("Dexter"* -TV Series, S6-E6: Showtime, 2012.)

Writing back in 650 BCE, Greek poet **Archilochus** divided people into two types: "hedgehogs" and "foxes". He noted that *"the fox knows many things, but the hedgehog knows one big thing"*. Even though the fox is very resourceful, he is powerless in front of the hedgehog's one and only strategy.

Specialists (the "hedgehogs" of this world) go deep in one thing, becoming the best in the world at that. Don't ask much else from them: they do *that* one thing really, really well —and that's pretty much it.

Multitalented people on the other hand... well, we have a broader perspective, many ideas, and lots of different interests. We have a natural inclination for many things and not enough time to do them all. Like 21st century da Vinci's, we love (and are generally pretty good at) several different, unrelated activities. Arts, handwork, writing, golf, singing... you name it—we have done it, or we want to do it. And we learn fast.

But—there's always a "but"—inconstancy is the dark companion of those who try to follow too many roads at once.

Hedgehogs don't need elaborate plans: they aim for success. *What do we foxes aim for?*

This book is for the person who suspects it is precisely our passion for *too many* things that sabotages our chances of accomplishment in any of them. **If we are changing paths all the time, we are not going anywhere, really.** Has that realization crossed your mind yet?

But among those hundred "passions" there is one *mission (or maybe two)* waiting to be uncovered. If we truly are foxes, we might as well use our cleverness to follow its scent, track down its path, and hunt it down, once and for all.

Enjoy!

Leo Lospennato, Berlin, 2012

(A Very Short) Introduction

[Battle School. Six-year-old Ender Wiggin—humanity's secret last hope against the incoming invasion of the same aliens that almost wiped the planet last time—is at risk of being killed by a bigger boy who feels threatened by Ender's abilities].

[Colonel GRAFF] *Ender must believe that no matter what happens, no adult will ever, ever step in to help him in any way. If he does not believe that, then he will never reach the peak of his abilities.*

[General PACE] *God help you if you're wrong.*

[Colonel GRAFF] *God help us all if I'm wrong.*

(From "Ender's Game", novel by Orson Scott Card).

What this book is not about

This is *not* a self-help book, although you will be reading it for your benefit, of course, as you would any book. The few experiences I will tell you about are my own, or of people I know; there are no imaginary "Eileen's" or "Joe's" stories in here.

This is *not* a New Age book. It contains no "Secrets" or other forms of wishful thinking. If anything, I will criticize simplistic solutions.

This is not a book on psychology, but it often refers to what eminent psychologists have discovered.

This is not a time management book, but it contains some concrete advice in that sense. Time management should only starts once you have decided how you will distribute your time among all the things you'd like to do: that's what this book is about.

This book, finally, is not an academic work. It is as serious and as exhaustive as I could make it, but is not formal or rigorous; it contains opinions, not theses. I had fun writing it; I want you to have fun reading it.

What this book is about

This book is about finding a portfolio of activities that reflects your inclinations, talents, and opportunities for profit.

This book is for the person with many talents, multiple passions, contradictory interests, raging bursts of enthusiasm that seem to go away as fast as they came, and the feeling that she hasn't yet found what she's been looking for.

If you feel identified with the description of the multitalented person I will offer two pages down, then I am sure you will enjoy this book.

By the time you finish the book, you should have:

- A clear landscape of your *real* interests and how they relate to each other and to your life.
- An understanding of which of those are vital and which are trivial.
- A decision regarding the degree of involvement you will go for on each of them.
- A big-picture plan to carry on with the things that matter, in the order they matter.
- An enjoyable reading experience!

I am far from being a life example for anyone; this book is a way to share my personal thoughts and findings, so I am sure you will not agree with everything written here. Simply take those passages with a grain of salt and keep enjoying the read.

So, here we go

There are no adults to step in to help us anymore. No parents, teachers, bosses, gurus, therapists, or priests who know which direction we must take. The only ones who know, somewhere deep inside, are us. If we don't believe that to the core of our souls, we will never reach the peak of our abilities.

PART I

(Where we figure out
what's going on with us
and what needs to be done.)

1

The Da Vinci Curse:
Signs, Causes, Dangers

[ALEX FLETCHER (Hugh Grant), a famous 1980s pop-music "has-been"—and now struggling solo artist—got commissioned to compose a new hit song for Cora Corman, the biggest star in today's pop scene. Incapable of writing any decent lyrics himself, he convinced SOPHIE FISHER (Drew Barrymore), a young woman who waters his plants, of using her fabulous but unexplored talent as songwriter to help him. After hours of sitting around in his living room not even one word has been written. SOPHIE intends to stop trying].

[ALEX] *What, are you leaving?!*

[SOPHIE] *Yes, sorry. Maybe I'll think of something later.*

[ALEX] *There is no "later". Cora needs the song tomorrow. If we don't give it to her, she's gonna go to someone else. I will have lost the job.*

[SOPHIE] *I'm sorry. I want to help. I do. I wanna help you finish, but I can't. I can't write when I feel like this. I'm not inspired!*

[ALEX] *I don't care! I don't care if you're inspired! Inspiration is for amateurs!*

From "Music and Lyrics", directed by Marc Lawrence, 2007.

Many people simply carry on with their lives in a dull, predictable fashion. Be born, go to school, work, marry, work, have children, work, retire, move to Florida, die.

Not us. We get depressed at the simple thought of that. We are under the same curse that affected da Vinci: we have many talents and interests, but only one life.

Leonardo da Vinci (1452—1519) is the classic example of a multitalented person and the quintessential "Renaissance man": painter, sculptor, architect, musician, scientist, mathematician, engineer, inventor, anatomist, geologist, cartographer, botanist, writer... Someone with "unquenchable curiosity" and a "feverishly inventive imagination".

The typical **Da Vinci-cursed** (a "**DVC**", from now on) is someone that shares that same spirit. A person who:

- Loves the world and all kinds of things in it.
- Has a fine aesthetic sensibility that allows her to enjoy art, music, exploration, science, and innumerable other activities.
- Has (or has had) a lot of hobbies: philately, martial arts, and whatnot.
- Has changed careers more than once, or longs to do so.

Some of us have realized that it is already too late for some fantasies. If you wanted to be a world-class violinist and you are 30 or more, you don't stand a chance. In fact, in this competitive world you don't stand a chance even if you were 15. You should have started at 6 or 7, like Paganini or Mozart did, with no guarantees at all that you would reach their level.

But, what 7-year old knows that *one* thing he wants to do for the rest of his life, anyway? Any normal kid, at 7, dreams of being a starship commander, a lion hunter and the town's sheriff, all at the same time. Behind Mozart and Paganini's extraordinary musical proficiency hide stories of abusive parents forcing them to perform beyond what any kid deserves.

However, the "child prodigy" profile (single-talented and highly specialized from an early age on) has nothing to do with us. We are the exact opposite:

1. We are not kids anymore.
2. We live in a time in which discoveries are not made by individuals but by highly professional, corporate-funded teams (the boss of the team takes the Nobel and the pharmaceutical company takes the patent).
3. We DVC's are not geniuses in *one* particular area, but people with above average talent and interest in *several*.

I believe that multitalented people don't actually have *many* talents: they have a few fundamental ones that are the base for all the others. They learn fast, they are curious, and they have a good memory. These talents are at the same time incredibly valuable and not always compatible with the persistence and discipline required to achieve success in today's world. "Hedgehogs" are precisely set on the bull's-eye; we "foxes" try to hit too many targets at the same time.

Is it "normal" to have multiple, apparently incompatible, wishes in adult life?

Of course it is. Knowledge of the world is not accessible only to the upper classes anymore. In ancient times, no one but a privileged few could write and read; nowadays anyone living in the free world can google up anything she wants to find out more about. But unlike the kid who fantasizes about adventures in outer space, the jungle, and the Far West all at the same time, we as adults have the chance—and the need—to anchor our dreams to the real world.

Is there hope for us of being happy in a world that rewards specialization?

It depends. It depends on your expectations. We cannot satisfy all the demands of our narcissistic selves. We may never win an Oscar or be president, but if we, as mature adults, are ready to interpret and outgrow those inner-child fantasies, we may just yet find that thing in life "especially made for us," an activity that will summon and challenge our strongest talents and inclinations. An activity that actually feels like a *mission*. We might never get to be astronauts or *concertinos*, but there is good news: many talents can *only* flourish by reaching maturity.

Let me tell a story related to music. A guy from my hometown was studying to be a doctor. After suffering an episode of mental fatigue, it was recommended that he stop for a while and use his time on strictly recreational activities. He started playing piano from scratch, and ended up being a soloist and a trainer specialized in forming other soloists. He currently spends 6 months in Argentina and 6 months in Los Angeles. He also finished his medical training and became a psychiatrist.

Another case: a young man who played professional basketball in the top division of a team called *Ferrocarril Oeste*, one of the best in South America. He abandoned the team the moment he realized he didn't enjoy the game anymore. After some time wandering in confusion about what to do with his life, some friends invited him to a concert of classical music, and he became infatuated with the cello. He trained for a few years, moved to Spain, and today plays the cello in several orchestras in Barcelona. He's not a Pau Casals or a Yo-Yo Ma, and he doesn't need to. He's just happy making a living out of what he loves.

These are not unusual DVC stories. We have the talent, the enthusiasm, the dreams, and sometimes we may have the opportunities too.

So what's missing?

The sign of The Cursed

Having many talents and interests is a trait, not a health condition. But its signs are not pretty. We may frequently experience:

- **A sense of shallowness.** We feel "Jacks of all trades and masters of none".
- **A sense of time loss.** Time goes by and we haven't found what "we were born to do".

- **A sense of failure.** Our childhood expectations (parent-imposed or self-imposed—it doesn't matter much now) are nowhere near becoming a reality. Not many astronaut positions openings are available for middle-aged, slightly overweight, multitalented people, are they? (Don't worry; chances are you would hate being an astronaut, anyway).

However, the feelings listed above have a precise function, one we will expose and understand.

Causes of the DVC

Who or what made us like this? Why can't we just find our life's passion and follow it? I think it is precisely because of our above-average palette of resources. The more options we have, the harder is to choose. Or maybe is something more on the negative side: maybe we truly are inconstant and dilettantes. Maybe. Maybe were discouraged when we were children, so now we keep looking for that one, perfect thing that will finally prove them wrong.

Education might have a role, too. Education dislocates many people from their natural talents. Our resources (just like natural resources) are often buried deep; they do not just lay around on the surface—the proper circumstances for them to reveal themselves have to be created. Maybe the education we received forced us to adapt to standard contents, not exploring our natural inclinations and talents, or things sufficiently complex and deep as to satisfy our uncommon personalities.

Teachers know little about the labor market and what is involved in different types of jobs; kids jump from schools to jobs with few or no opportunities to take part in work experience. Few employers are invited to the school to talk to students; career fairs are scarce and career guidance services are not standard part of school structures. And if guidance services exist, they lack resources, specific training, and coordinated work with teachers and parents.

Whatever the cause, we have become chronic avoiders of the conflict that true mastery demands. We have been jumping from piano lessons to Spanish lessons to Tae-Kwon-Do lessons; we have yet to find our path in this hyper-specialized world, and defiantly walk it.

Leaving wishful thinking behind

Let's get back to ancient Greece for a second. The so called *cynics* were a school of thought founded by Socrates's disciples back in the 5th century BCE. Their philosophy described a life of virtue in agreement with Nature, rejecting all conventional desires for wealth, power, and fame. They went a little too far down that road, though, to the point of also rejecting all possessions. But there is something interesting in that philosophy: the word 'cynic' comes from the Greek expression for 'dog-like': a style of confronting life without much regard for embellishments.

I believe that the DVC problem has been approached by several authors as if the core of the matter was to feel better with ourselves—an approach, unlike the cynics' way, *full* of embellishments and consolations:

- *"Refuse to choose; do everything you love"*. On the contrary, I am convinced that we have to choose wisely. We cannot afford to do everything we want; most of it would be a loss of time, taking our focus away from the significant things in our lives. We would be dividing our time among so many activities to the point of not doing anything, really—at least not seriously. No: let's consider options, let's choose carefully and intelligently, and let's follow the one path we are called to follow. The rest are merely hobbies.

- *"Accept yourself as you are"*. That's fine in principle. But what if "what we are" is not "what we want to (or must) be"? Our duty is to transform ourselves, to *become*, not just accept what we *became*.

- *"Start small, start right now."* And then what? Quit as always, after a few weeks? No. I propose to plan things first, and *then* start. And

I believe that more important than "to start" is "to stay" through the first difficulties.

- *"Don't bother to finish any of it"*. Seriously? (I did read that in a book, actually). Not finishing things leaves us short-changed. Reaching milestones, instead, gives us a sense of accomplishment. You don't need to get a PhD in everything you start, but there is no point in starting something without intending to draw some value from it.

Much in the fashion of the old cynics, I propose —instead of consoling ourselves with self-help books and medicating our frustrations— to take an honest look at our problem: inconstancy, drifting, and dissatisfaction. Let's not find a way *around* that, but the way through it.

A matter of life and death (no kidding)

Individuation (also called **self-actualization**) is an alignment between our "self" (our *ego*, that person we call *"I"*) and our "Self".

What is this "Self" (big "S")? It is the inner agency clamoring for corrective action in the direction of our lives:

- The religious believer might interpret it as "the voice of God within".

- The skeptical, non-religious person may interpret it as a growing inner impulse; an emergence stemming from processes ultimately physical in nature, but increasingly influencing our conscious thoughts.

- Jungian psychology defines it as the most important archetype, the center around which our whole psychological life structures itself.

In ascending order of intensity, these are the ways our "Self" demands of us a change of path:

- **Fantasies and longings,** which help us escape the present.

- **Dreams.** In particular, those whose message can be interpreted as "you are going the wrong way!"

- **Nightmares**. Dreams of especial intensity, demanding particular attention in that way.

- **Increasing physical ailments.** Forced inauthenticity may remain unconscious, yet it engenders profound suffering that one may somaticize as illness.

- If it has to come to it: **personality disorders (neuroses).** The inner call *will* manifest itself, no matter how quiet we want it to remain. In the words of the eminent psychologist Carl G. Jung, *"the function of neuroses is no different from the function of dreams—only rather more forceful and drastic"*.

- If it really, really has to come to it (and sorry if this sounds too dramatic): ***physical death.***

Don't believe it? Jung himself warns us about it:

> If the demand for self-knowledge [of a man] is refused, this negative attitude may end in real death. Only self-knowledge can extricate him; if he refuses this, then no other way is left open. Usually he is not conscious of his situation, so he is at the mercy of unforeseen dangers: he cannot get out of the way of a car quickly enough; in climbing a mountain he misses his foothold somewhere; out skiing he thinks he can negotiate a tricky slope, and in an illness he suddenly loses the courage to live. The unconscious has a thousand ways of snuffing out a meaningless existence with surprising swiftness.

But even if you don't end up getting killed in a ski accident, what awaits for us in the future? This is what **José Mujica**, president of Uruguay, foresees:

My fellow workers have long battled to have their work day limited to 8 hours. And now they are succeeding in getting it limited to 6 hours. But then they get two jobs, and end up working more than before. Why? Because they have to pay installments: the little motorbike they bought, the little car they bought... Paying installments, paying installments... and before they know, each of them has become an old, rheumatic person like me—someone who realizes that his life is already gone.

Ignoring the demands of the Self

Instead of living a simpler, more austere life, we struggle the wrong way for the wrong things. We have bad jobs to pay for things we don't need, using up our time instead of enjoying the activities and the people we love. We don't give them our time; we give them iPhones and PlayStations that we pay for by being away from home 50, 60, or more hours in order to avoid downsizings and to hunt for managerial positions that generate even more workload.

And once we get home, we need to "relax" by using:

- **The Networks.** Pathetic shopping-TV programs; social networks filled with kittens' pictures and *"meh"* jokes; celebrity-starred "reality" shows; news channels that repeat the same news again and again, and infinite sit-com re-runs.

- **The junk:** Materialism run amok, expressed by must-have SUV's, TV-sets, espresso machines, audio systems, computers, or smartphones. God forbid our "friends" may look down on us because our Apple gizmo is the model "5" instead of "6".

- **The substances:** if the inner call won't stay put, we drown it with alcohol, we hide it in smoke, we stuff food in "its" mouth, distract it with pornography, or worst.

Why do we insist on ignoring the internal "call" to pursue another life, a life more aligned with our real interests and talents?

- **Because we haven't interpreted that call as such**, and we attribute our symptoms to any variety of psychological or organic causes.

- **Because we think we cannot follow that call.** We are simply not leaving the security of our job in order to start a new professional project, especially if this may impact the financial stability of a family that depends on us. This is, of course, a legitimate concern.

- **Because we are afraid of following it.** Because following our dreams will upset someone else or threaten the dynamics of that relationship.

- **Because we could pass someone up.** Men (in particular but not exclusively) must confront a bitter alternative in their lives: 1) either not reaching the "level" their fathers reached—establishing a setback in the lineage— or 2) surpassing that level. Men unconsciously model their lives after their father's, so passing them up means to step into uncharted territory.

- **Just "because"**—which means we simply ignore the reasons behind our unproductive past-times, addictions and/or materialistic pursues by reasons that are still not very clear to us.

Complex, long-term problems do not have short-term answers. Facing a potential life or career change is a process that needs careful planning and smart execution, breaking patterns of inconstancy and dispersion, and other things easier said than done.

Tests "don't pass the test"

What is the supposed "mission" of your life? What is that magical activity you've been circling around as long as you can recall?

Well, first of all, it's not magical at all, unless your dream is to be appointed professor at Hogwarts. Second, that mission may be something you already did, or do (although some adjustments might be in order).

Third, it does not necessarily have to be a job, a profession, or a business. In this book, we will frequently discuss the financial dimension of our potential endeavors, but it can also be something not-for-profit: a purely amateur activity, a humanitarian initiative, a voluntary endeavor. This is especially valid for those in their older years or with their financial needs already resolved.

Fourth, the mission of one's life *has* to be something much more complex and well defined than vocational and personality tests suggest. Tests don't pass the test, because:

- If they are based on *aptitudes* (*"You are 66% accountant, 33% architect"*), their results will be not necessarily aligned with our *wishes*.
- If on the contrary they are based only on wishes and not aptitudes or chances of making money, they are simply wishful thinking.
- If they do not take into account your personality and your preferences regarding work environment (indoors vs. outdoors, alone vs. in team, etc.), they are simply *not us*.

Since we are quoting Jung, take for example the MTBI test ("Myers-Briggs Type Indicator" test), probably the most popular personality test out there. Most sources I have consulted during my research for this book sooner or later refer the reader to the MTBI. However, some academic psychologists have criticized the test, claiming lack of convincing validity data, lack of statistical validity and low reliability. Plus, the use of the MTBI as a predictor of job success has not been supported in studies; in fact, such use is expressly discouraged by the authors of the test themselves. You can take the test online, if you want. The result will tell you which one of 16 different personality types you belong to, according to your preferred ways of thinking and acting. It will not tell you what it is that you have been looking for, and it probably will tell you much of what you already know.

As for career tests, they follow the "trait-and-factor" theory: they 1) study the individual, 2) survey occupations, 3) match them. The problem is that they do not account for how interests, values, aptitudes, achievement, and personalities grow and change; they assume a unique pattern of abilities and traits that can be objectively measured, and people do not conform so easily to such description, much less us DVC's.

No. We are talking about something much more profound here. Not simply about career aptitude, not just about generalities about our personalities, not just about time-management. We are talking about something related to who we are, not merely what we could *do* to some degree of probability.

Consequently, our "mission-to-be" will likely be:

- **Not simple** but complex, because that is the way we look at the world.

- **Not common,** but somehow special, because DVC's are not average; traditional things do not satisfy them or exploit the best in them.

- **Not mundane,** but something *meaningful.*

And for once, whether you are inspired or not is not that important. More important is whether you are ready to *perspire:* we have still many pages to go —all easy to understand, some of them not easy to read.

2

The Age Of Specialization: Living In A Vertical World

[JOHN WATSON (Martin Freeman) is brought to an undisclosed place to meet a mysterious MAN (Mark Gatiss). WATSON refuses to sit, despite his difficulty standing—he got shot in the war in Afghanistan. He doesn't know nor trust the man in front of him].

[MAN] I imagine people have already warned you to stay away from Sherlock Holmes, but I can see from your left hand that's not going to happen.

[WATSON] What's wrong with my hand?

[MAN] You have an intermittent tremor in your left hand. Your therapist thinks it's a post-traumatic stress disorder. She thinks you're haunted by memories of your military service.

[WATSON] Who the hell are you? How do you know all that?

[MAN] Fire her. She's got it the wrong way round. You are under stress right now and your hand is perfectly steady. You are not haunted by the war: you miss it. Welcome back. Time to choose a side, Dr. Watson.

(From "Sherlock — A Study in Pink" — BBC, 2010.)

Human endeavors are born as ideas.

It all starts as an inspiring, crazy *"what if?"* Then it becomes *experiment*, which generates *knowledge*. If it is viable, it becomes *design* (a plan, a program, a description). Then, it becomes a product (this includes services, immaterial things like software, songs, internet access, charities, taxi rides, and everything else we might need).

Take, for example, the iPhone. The development of that product (since it started as a drawing on a napkin, going all the way to one's pocket) involved different areas of knowledge with different actors. Check if you feel identified with any of these roles:

- The **philosophers** of the field, the "visionaries". In Apple that person was Steve Jobs, or whoever imagined a new Apple product in the hands of their customers when neither of them existed. This is where the conceptual grounds for a discipline are set: an activity normally limited to solitary disquisitions, academic contexts, or the secrecy of corporate strategy meetings.

- The **scientists** of the field. This is where the validation of the new paradigm happens. Working in this phase of an endeavor implies using highly abstract logic and mathematical language (anything deserving of being called "a science" is based on logic and/or math), and even creating new scientific tools able to explore those foundational ideas.

- Going up you have the **designers**, people who shape those abstract ideas into real world specifications. Some discovery of—say—an electrostatic field distortion find its way into a new iPad's touch screen: designers transform scientific principles into practical ends.

- **Engineers** take those specifications and make them work: they transform a blueprint into a real iPad. Yes, "nerd" is the new "hot".

- Now, someone has to coordinate and organize all these people and their resources; someone has to make sure the organization is financially sustainable, that no laws are being infringed, that everyone stays satisfied with their jobs, and that there's a serious business going on—these are the organizers, the **managers.**

- But the ones who know how to transform a product into a cult object are the **marketers**—so Apple (the company that hires all the people described above) can become a top Fortune-500 company.

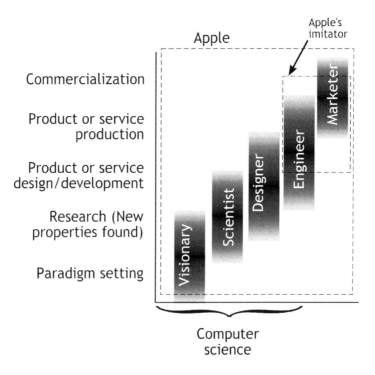

Fig. 1: Different roles in the development of a product like the iPhone.

- If something is not done according to the law, the **observers** (reporters, critics, writers, attorneys) will notice and demand corrective action; otherwise the **enforcers** (police, judges, etc.) will have to intervene.
- Every level of the organization has people teaching, training, and helping others to better do their jobs: they are the **supporters** (trainers, technicians, janitors, doctors, etc.)
- Later on, the **artists** will take that story and make it into a book, a movie, a comic strip or a song.

All this to drop on you the sad truth that we DVC's have to confront: **The world belongs to the *specialists*.**

Back in da Vinci's time it was the opposite way. Those with wider knowledge could lead (teach, influence, command, rule upon) or become a valuable resource for the power in place—to kings and other nobility, for whom the empowering resource was *ancestry* and the associated financial and military strength.

Had da Vinci lived in our times, he would have wanted to invent, design, and build a computer way cooler than the iPad; he would have wanted to be the CEO of Da Vinci Enterprises, Inc., and he would had made a movie about it all, filmed with a camera invented by him. But he would have lost the "pad" competition to Apple, the Oscar to Spielberg, and the camera market to Panasonic, for in today's world we can embrace knowledge in several fields only by resigning depth in all of them.

Until a few years ago, a good option for people with many talents and interests was to become managers—a career that allowed them to have competence in different areas of an organization. But that paradigm went extinct. Today's managers are highly specialized, too: specialized in management, of course. The different areas they oversee are dealt with as black boxes: inputs, outputs, costs, and returns on investment. Numbers. "Human Resources" managers are no exception, so please let go of the idea that the HR department of your company is responsible or even remotely interested in *your* professional development. Employees are not taken care of anymore, like they were in older times. Companies now consider employees as *consultants*: it is the employees who must bring the knowledge and expertise to the organization—not the other way around.

No place for know-it-alls

A person can reasonably expect to reach excellence in *one* phase of *one* area of human knowledge. The limits of their competence become grayer, thinner, as they move away from their narrow, vertical niches of expertise. Know-it-alls are outmoded, for two main reasons:

1. People don't like know-it-alls.
2. Being a true know-it-all is an impossibility.

The volume of the world's data doubles every few years; no matter how fast we learn, it will always scale to practically nothing compared with the explosive growth of the world's knowledge and how easy to get it is.

Imagine the following dialog. Someone says to you, *"I am involved in the production of Swiss cheese"* (this is a normal person, not some know-it-all). In order to understand what she does, we *have* to ask her *"what do you mean, 'Swiss cheese'? Production, degustation, distribution, the milk, the cows…?"*

"Oh, my work in the countryside near Bern is focused on the cows", she says. And again, we ask: *"What do you mean, 'cows'? Breeding, milking, nutrition? Or maybe are you a veterinarian?"*

"Yes", she says, "I'm a vet". And we refrain from asking about her specialty (surgery, reproduction, parasitology, etc.) simply not to look too inquisitive.

Switzerland as a whole certainly knows a lot about cheese (and about banking, watches and chocolates, too). But they lack a space program, among other things. One of the first concepts they teach you in marketing class is that no organization can be *everything* to all its customers: the organization has to find its niche both in terms of *what* it offers, and *to whom* it offers it. So you see, not even entire organizations or nations can afford to be know-it-alls; consequently, the thought of a person trying to be an expert in *everything* is just ludicrous.

You get the idea: **The less specialized you are, the farther you are from the top of a given field or market.**

Allow me to share a modest personal experience. I wrote the first-book-ever on one particular subject: electric guitars design. Consider how specific that is: the book is not about "music" nor is it about "musical instruments". It is not even about "guitars". It is specifically about *electric* guitars. And only about their design. Not construction, not history, not critique, not marketing. It had to be specific. And that is the reason why my book was the very first on the subject: In today's world, being specific is the only chance of being original.

So, what should we DVC people do? Should we go against our inclinations and abilities, against our wish of exploring the infinite things the world has to offer?

Should we repress our curiosity? Should we limit ourselves to one tiny, specific area of knowledge?

The answer to those questions is a resounding "Not in a million years".

Choose your poison

We have a choice. On one hand we have:

- Conformism ("do the easy thing to do").
- Victimization ("do what others want you to do").
- Inertia ("keep doing the same").

And, on the other hand, we have the chance of:

- Exploring our talents, wishes, and possibilities.
- Planning how to make them happen.
- Facing our own resistance and other obstacles.
- Finding a way to make our complex personality work in this vertical world, and to become not only satisfied but *self-actualized, truly individuated* in the process.

In our heart of hearts, we are spoiling for a fight with destiny. So, welcome to the fight. Time to choose a side.

3

The Answer To Life, The Universe, And Everything

[FOOQ and LOONQWILL, trans-dimensional beings, visit DEEP THOUGHT again after 7.5 million years. DEEP THOUGHT, the most powerful supercomputer ever created, spent that time calculating The Answer To Life, The Universe, And Everything, and it finally reached an answer. A huge, celebrating crowd follows the ceremony].

[DEEP TOUGHT]   *Alright. The answer to the Ultimate Question...*

[THE CROWD CHEERS IN EXPECTATION]

[DEEP TOUGHT]   *... of Life, the Universe, and Everything...*

[DEEP TOUGHT]   *... is...* [CHEERING IS AT ITS CLIMAX]

[DEEP TOUGHT]   *... Forty-Two.*

[THE CROWD, STUNNED, COMES TO AN ABRUPT SILENCE. FINALLY, SOMEONE SCREAMS:]

Forty-two???!!!

[DEEP TOUGHT]   *Yes, yes, I checked it thoroughly... It's forty-two. It would have been simpler, of course, to have known what the actual question was.*

[LOONQWILL]   *But it was THE Question! The Ultimate Question!*

[DEEP TOUGHT]   *That was not a question. Only when you know the actual question will you understand what the answer means.*

(From *"Hitchhiker's Guide to the Galaxy"*, directed by G. Jennings, 2005.)

I chose to start this chapter with that dialog from *Hitchhiker's* because it answers with fantasy, imagination, and a sense of humor the biggest question: *"What is the meaning to life?"*

"Forty-two" is a senseless answer, of course, but that's only because the question is senseless, too.

Please allow me to consider this matter with as much logic as a transcendental question can bear. The question about the meaning of life can be broken into three simpler questions.

1. Where we do come from?
2. What happens after we die?
3. What is the reason, or the meaning, of our existence in between?

Questions 1 and 2 are surprisingly easy to answer.

For religious people, the answers are: 1) "God", and 2) some form of eternal, spiritual life after death.

For secular people, the answer to question 1 ("where do we come from?") is "*supernovae*": Complex elements formed in the core of stars and were ejected to eventually form a type "M" planet suited for biogenesis and evolution. And the answer for question 2 ("*where do we go after we die?*") is "*nowhere*". When something ends, it ends.

Now, for question 3. What is the reason and purpose of our personal, individual existence? The answer is not so simple. Note that the question is not about the afterlife, but about *this* life.

Let me start clearing the area. The answer to the meaning of our life, *this* life, **cannot** adopt any of the following forms:

- **The Old Testament answer: To perpetuate life, "to be fruitful and multiply".** In short: "to procreate". What about people with no children who contributed to the world in ways much more significant than just giving birth to yet *more* people? Was procreating the "contribution" of Hitler's, Stalin's, and Idi Amin's mothers? Certainly not.

- **The "Darwinian" answer:** *"The meaning of life is to evolve"*. I think that the prospect of being just another link between a *Pithe-*

cus and the future trans-humans doesn't sound very exciting, nor "personal".

- **The Zen answer:** "To become one with the infinite" (or "eternity", "nothingness", "energy", "the universe", "the whole", etc.) How is that exactly supposed to happen, anyway?

Let me go a little deeper on this last one. The concept of "infinity", or "eternity", poses an intractable problem, because those are not comprehensible concepts. "Infinity" is not just "an incredibly long time".

I have read somewhere about a mental exercise to try to grasp the concepts of infinity and eternity, which goes like this:

> Imagine a ball of steel the size of the Earth. Imagine that once every trillion years a fly touches the ball with one of its wings. When the friction of the fly's wing has worn the ball down to nothing, infinity hasn't even begun.

Whichever number, no matter how big, is infinitesimal, it is *nothing at all* in comparison with infinity. Since we cannot derive meaning from the incomprehensible, *no meaning* can be derived from an infinite existence. Bear with me in this thought: Eternity cannot be the answer to life, because an eternal life cannot have meaning. All our acts would lose signification and relevance. A few millennia here, a few trillion years there... an eternal being is either condemned to permanent change (loosing individuality, personality, and choice—becoming something else entirely)—or is condemned to eternal repetition: a routine that unavoidably copies itself for ever and ever.

Our minds cannot wrap around the concept of infinity, and the same goes for nothingness, pure energy, and other New-Age, rather vague concepts. Living forever in some undefined energy form doesn't sound comforting to me, and such a prospect doesn't solve our search for meaning *here* and *now*. If anything, *finitude* is the meaning-giver.

Also, "to seek peace"; "to expand our conscience"; "to contribute to the well-being and spirit of others"…. These answers do not work for me. I want to know the meaning of my life, of *this* life. Gurus and preachers are entitled to express their opinions about the meaning of their lives (even though such opinions sound dangerously like dogma); they don't get to decide such matter for others. What the heck do they know?

Cynical answers

These are the answers not of the Greek cynics but of the *cynical*, people who distrust other's motives and lack faith in the human race and life in general. They go like this: *"Life is a bitch, and then you freaking die"*, which is a rude way to say *"the question is too profound, too complex to be understood"*.

Well, no. I understand the question well. Maybe the answer is too profound, but the question is a pretty simple one.

Of course, we can always deny the problem. We can (wrongly, in my opinion) say:

- *"Life simply has no meaning."*
- *"Life or human existence has no real meaning or purpose because it occurred out of a random chance in nature; ergo, it has no intended purpose."*
- *"Life has no meaning, but we humans ascribe meaning or purpose to it so we can justify our existence, or make it more bearable."*
- *"One should not seek to know and understand the meaning of life. Because."*
- *"Don't think about that. You will never live if you are looking for the meaning of life. The meaning of life is to forget about the search for the meaning of life."*

Yes, we can just hide our heads in a hole and ignore or deny the problem. Not that such a thing is going to work, of course. If anything, it is going to make things worse.

Plus, denying the problem is a lost opportunity to find sanity:

> [The] search for meaning may arouse inner tension rather than inner equilibrium. However, precisely such tension is an indispensable prerequisite of mental health.

Kurt Gödel (1906-1978), was one of the greatest logicians and mathematicians of the 20th Century; he fled his native Austria to avoid the expanding Nazi regime in Europe. Gödel was the author of the theorem that carries his name (also called the "incompleteness theorem"), which proves that some truths cannot be stated as such in the same theoretic frame in which the proposition was originally made.

The theorem was of course intended for use in a formal-logic realm; it cannot be lightly taken out of context to be applied in relation to the meaning of life. However, I find interesting that another Austrian contemporary with Gödel—the philosopher **Ludwig Wittgenstein**—thought that the question about the meaning of life turns out to be unsolvable (i.e. meaningless) within the logical realm in which it is posed to us—*language*. In his *Philosophical Remarks,* Wittgenstein confirms:

> The meaning of a question is the method of answering it. Tell me how are you searching, and I will tell you what you are searching for.

So, you see: the answer to the question about the meaning of life *can* be given, but just not in words. In order to be effectively given, the question needs to exist in a realm other than language. That realm is *action*, which is another word for "life".

Ask a chess master "what is the best chess move?" and enjoy the expression of confusion in his face. No such thing exists, of course. The same holds for human existence, but we keep asking the question, nonetheless. At best, the only answer that can be given is the favorite answer of engineers to anything you ask them: *"well, it depends"*. It is not the answer that's wrong. The *realm* in which we are trying to give that answer is. The incompleteness theorem applies here: we can talk for ages about the matter, but nothing we say will resolve the question. Language just won't do, because the core of the question is not symbolic or imaginary (like language is), but *real*.

The limit of symbols

The symbols '5 + 7 = 12' have a meaning because they *represent* something. They are an abstraction; the numbers in the equation represent hats, ants, cars, or whatever you are referring to. Five galaxies plus seven galaxies equals twelve galaxies. It is incredible that some stains of ink on a paper can help "manipulate" objects of astronomical dimension, isn't it? In that simplicity resides the power of representation.

'Meaning' is synonymous with 'representing'. We use something (symbols or signs) to represent something else (an object, idea, data, notion) for reasons of economy, simplicity, practicality, or communication. When you say the words *'my life'*, you point not to a thing, but to a process: your life. That is the meaning (the allusion) made by the words 'my life'. But your *actual* life does not re-present anything. It *presents* something, instead: it presents itself.

Consider the word 'tree'. When you read it, an image of a tree—some tree—comes to your mind. The word *tree* is symbolic (the *signifier*); the image formed in your mind is imaginary (the *signified*), and the tree you see when you look out the window (the tree *itself*, not the image of that tree in your retinas) is *real*.

Life is like the real-tree. Not the word 'life'; not what you understand when you read the word 'life', not your understanding of your life, but your *real* life. It is what it is, and it does not intend to symbolize anything. Consequently, **it has *no* meaning *per se*.**

Does that mean that life is meaningless? Well, it depends.

Victor Frankl (1905-1997) was a neurologist and psychiatrist as well as a Holocaust survivor. Frankl was the founder of logotherapy—a form of existential analysis—and is a prominent source of inspiration for humanistic psychologists. His bestseller *Man's Search for Meaning* chronicles his experiences as a concentration camp inmate and describes his psychotherapeutic method of finding meaning in all situations of existence. Frankl's is not just another book: A survey conducted by the U.S. Library of Congress puts it among the ten most influential books in the United States—ever. On page 122 of my copy, it says:

> Man's search for meaning is the primary motivation in his life and not a "secondary rationalization" of instinctual drives. This meaning is unique and specific in that it must and can be fulfilled by him alone; only then it achieves a significance which will satisfy his own will to meaning.

So, if the question "what is the meaning of life" makes no real sense, the closer we can get to a correctly posed question would be: "What is the meaning of what I am *doing* right now for me (and for those whom I care about)?"

Again, words fall short, somehow.

Action, not words

The question about the meaning of life must be reconstructed not as a question, but as an answer, expressed in a realm that transcends language: action.

We thought *we* were the ones *asking* the question, but actually we are the ones *being asked*. You are the one who has to answer to life—not with words, but with your life. In short:

- Imperfection, limitations and finitude are *essential* to meaning. Perfection and infinitude don't have any boundaries and consequently cannot provide meaning, because meaning is all about differentiating, putting limits and direction to something.

- Frustration and dissatisfaction are, paradoxically, the very triggers of the search for meaning.

- The meaning of life makes no sense as a question. Life is maybe nonsense; but if we don't live its nonsense and at least try to unravel it, we will never have lived at all.

The answer (not in words, but in action) can have one of these forms:

1. Experiencing something (goodness, beauty, truth in nature or culture) or finding someone (loving another human being).
2. The attitude we take toward unavoidable suffering. When it's our turn to be confronted with a hopeless situation we have the chance of transforming a personal tragedy into a triumph: we are challenged to change ourselves.
3. **By creating a work or doing a deed**.

This book deals with the third way. Note the words in it. "Creating". "Work". "Doing". "Deed". The obvious focus is on action.

We DVC's have been blessed with a lot of potentialities. But really, who cares if you *could* become a brilliant doctor or a great novelist? After all, if you could become something and you didn't, you are liable of not living up to your potential. But as soon as you finish your novel, or get your diploma, or open your small business your potential is *actualized*—is rendered a reality. It is, in Frankl's words, **safely delivered into the past.** It's in the bag, forever.

So, that's is the *Answer to life*: Life is not about finding meaning in it, is about *giving* meaning to it.

Now, the *Answer to the Universe and Everything* is even simpler.

It's "forty-two", of course.

4

Typical DVC: Avoidance, Inconstancy, Blockages

[NEO (Keanu Reeves), "The One", he who is supposed to save humanity from the uprising of the Machines, lays face down on the street after having been repeatedly beaten up by AGENT SMITH (Hugo Weaver) —an artificial, sentient, and evil entity. NEO makes a superhuman effort and barely succeeds in standing up again.]

[SMITH] *Why? Why do you do it? Why, why get up? Why keep fighting? Do you believe you're fighting for something, for more than your survival? Can you tell me what it is? Do you even know? Is it freedom, or truth, perhaps peace - could it be for love? Illusions, Mr. Anderson, vagaries of perception. You must be able to see it, Mr. Anderson; you must know it by now! You can't win; it is pointless to keep fighting! Why, Mr. Anderson, why, why do you persist?*

[NEO] [READY TO CONTINUE THE FIGHT] *Because I choose to.*

(From "The Matrix - Revolutions"

Directed by A. and L. Wachowski, 1999.)

"*When the going gets tough, the tough get going.*" But not us.

Nope. When the going gets though, multitalented people just look for something else.

We experience intense waves of enthusiasm, but we are not able to keep going past the first barriers, long before we acquire any real dexterity in that field. We always change our minds regarding the things we want to do. And when an activity becomes too hard a challenge (the sign that we are about to transcend the level of beginners) we get "bored" and we resist to continue.

Leonardo Da Vinci was the epitome of inconstancy himself. **Giorgio Vasari**, da Vinci's first biographer, said about Leonardo:

> He talked much more about his works than he ever achieved. So many things were left unfinished: that was the fate of nearly all his projects. The Last Supper left unfinished; the Mona Lisa, incomplete after working on it for four years; for the friars of the Annunziata he never even began the altarpiece.

Even Pope Leo X said of him during the three years that they overlapped in Rome:

> This man will never do anything, for he begins to think of the end before the beginning.

It may serve as consolation that 500 years later we are still talking about "this man who will never do anything" as one of the greatest creators humankind has known.

I think that even when we DVC's don't finish things, we don't leave empty handed, either. People who drop from new activities after a few weeks (or days, or even hours) actually *do* accomplish something: whatever we were looking for is obtained early in the process, and then our interest vanishes. *What* has been satisfied right there and then? What did we "achieve" right before the moment we feel like leaving? See if you can recognize yourself in the one or more of the following options:

- **Feeling the thrill of discovery.** People who move pretty quickly between activities are just satisfying a transitory curiosity. We live in fascination. We hear a viola da gamba for the first time and infatuation ensues; some amazing fact about the Big Bang makes us feel that we were born to unravel the secrets of the universe, and so on. The appeal of new activities diminishes after the initial mysteries have been decoded, though; we start having second thoughts about it, afraid that we might be losing the chance to do something even better (i.e. fear of the "cost of opportunity").

- **Embellishing our personality.** We collect badges of experience. We can say: "I am such and such"—"*I am a karateka*", "*I am a guitar player*", or whatever. We persevere only until we are not *newbies* anymore; we are sort of embellishing our "know-it-all's *résumé*".

- **Verification of our own talents.** I found this funny equation somewhere:

    Modern Art = "Pfff—I can do that!" + "Yeah, but you didn't".

    Maybe we just want to reach a point at which we prove to ourselves that we could do it, like an exploration of your own limits. It is like saying: *"See? I could become a great archer!"* and then looking for the next challenge that confirms our extensive range of potentials.

- **Avoiding an investment of energy.** Maybe our early departure from hobbies and careers is just a strategy to avoid confronting the sacrifice that sooner or later arises in every endeavor before you actually master them.

- **Fear of competing with others.** In sports (but also in other disciplines), a good way to improve our skills is by confronting someone who is slightly better than us. But some people simply don't want to be exposed to defeat.

- **Rejecting the commitment that mastery requires.** Learning a new discipline or profession requires dedication: attending regular classes, regular practice, studying... Not getting serious is a way to keep our agenda free to jump around some more.

- **Becoming subject to evaluation from other people.** Maybe we are too sensitive to feedback; maybe we take ourselves too seriously. Maybe we haven't realized the elemental fact that we *must* start as students, never as masters—another sign of a big ego standing in our way.

- **Putting up a show.** To excel at something may take years, so maybe acquiring a cosmetic "aura" of mastery suffices. *"Oh, I am currently getting myself into Japanese culture of the XIII and XVI centuries. Very interesting".* Sometimes it works as a conversation opener with potential romantic partners. Sometimes is doesn't: clever people can see right through such cosmetic crap.

- **Blocked by theory, blocked by practice.** Some of us become fascinated with the logical, theoretical, philosophical foundations of things but lose interest when we must put them into practice. Or vice versa: we are doers, and lose interest in something as soon as we have to dive deeper into the theory in order to consolidate our advance.

Classic example: learning music. At 18 I became fascinated with classical music and started studying violin, an instrument that requires *a lot* of dedication and practice, not to mention learning how to read music. A couple of months later, I had already dropped the classes and was limited to a messy, unfocused fiddling in my room. Another month later, I was learning karate, or something. It was the effort required to master music theory that scared me away.

Not knowing what we want

Maybe we simply do not know what we want. We might think we are ultimately looking for *happiness*, but maybe we are not even looking for that. Contemporary cultural critic **Slavoj Žižek** says:

> Happiness is for me a much compromised category. People do not really want or desire happiness and I think that's a good thing. For example, when you are in a creative endeavor, in a wonderful fever, "oh my god, I am on to something" and so on, happiness doesn't enter: you are ready to suffer. Happiness is for me an unethical category.

And then he confirms the suspicion that we do not find a thing to stick to, because:

> We don't want what we think we want. [Consider] the typical misogynist scenario: I am married to my wife, my relations with her are cold and I have a mistress, and all the time I dream: "Oh my god, if my wife were to disappear somehow it would open up the chance of a life for me with my mistress". Do you know what every psychoanalyst will tell you that quite often happens? That if for some reason the wife goes away, you lose the mistress, too. It turns out that the situation was much more complex than you thought. You want to keep the mistress at a distance, as an object of desire about which you dream. I don't think this is an excessive situation; I think this is how things really work.

We want both (wife and mistress), and, at some level, we want none (since that's how things frequently end up). And maybe the same goes for other things in our lives. We want this, we want that, we want it all and we end up with nothing in particular. Each avoidance strategy —each made up excuse—yields a particular benefit: to save our fearful butts from the pains of confronting real life, the dominion in which *meaning* dwells.

Jumping into the chalk outline

Maybe we are fitting (or trying to fit) too well to the roles society expects from us. I believe this is especially true for women.

When we meet new people (in a party, for example) we try to form a quick picture of the kind of person we have in front of us. For men, the factor we perceive as the most defining of their personalities is their profession. *"What do you do?"* is the qualifying question. But in the case of a woman, if we could ask one question only, what we (right or wrong) perceive as more informative is her family status. If a woman is married or not, with children or not, divorced or not, lesbian or not... that is what we use as this person's picture. Such an attitude is of course *snob* (as author Alain de Botton puts it), because we take a small part of the life of a person and use that to come to a complete vision of who this person is.

And into that trap we jump. It's like someone draws the chalk outline of a body on the floor, and we just walk up and lay down in there, adopting the shapes that society (including us) has predefined.

Things are better in this sense now than 30 or 40 years ago. But we still define a person by their adaptation to the classic social roles, and we do the same thing with ourselves. But maybe we can change the game.

What lies at the other side of the wall?

These are some possible motivations for change:

- **To improve job satisfaction.** To work in contact with more people (or on the contrary, alone), or to change a cubicle-job for a more outdoorsy occupation (or vice versa). Bad bosses, bad schedules, bad companies... in short: bad jobs get changed to better ones every day.

- **To obtain recognition or social status.** What is the kind of recognition you want to obtain? Admiration, recognition of intelligence, respect, physical prowess, becoming desirable; or maybe some form of revenge? Paradoxically, a fulfilled person transmits a better image to the world, since less energy is spent in projecting appearances (possessions, titles, and vacation pictures on Facebook) and one's true personality can shine through: humor, creativity, and self-expression.

    As social beings, we not only need monetary currency, but also *social* currency. We need to be accepted by our peers, bosses, friends, lovers... That's natural and reasonable, unless we become so dependent on it that the opposite happens: we start losing the approval we desperately look for. Do we just want to make friends? To meet romantic partners? Chances are that for the person walking a definite path, recognition will arise spontaneously, instead of being "begged" for.

- **To leave a legacy**. The Jiminy Cricket within us asks: *"Why just pass through existence unnoticed, when we can leave our mark in the world?"*

- **To help others.** Maybe that "mark in the world" does not have the shape of a symphony, or other grandiose and ambitious expression. Maybe it has the form of other people receiving love, help, and hope from us —in whatever way we are most gifted to share that human touch.

- **To pursue happiness and meaning.** A moment arrives in which we don't want (or cannot afford without becoming ill) to live from weekend to weekend, vacation to vacation, and finding a temporary sense of accomplishment in buying things. At that point the options are reduced to: "to transform and suffer", or "*not* to transform and suffer even more".

- **For money.** Is it money what you want to achieve? That is not something bad, of course. Money doesn't buy happiness, but is a good tension reliever.

A word about money

Hundreds of books tell us *"you can be rich too"*, *"claim your wealth"*, etc. Scientific studies, indeed, do show a direct relation between money and happiness. But interestingly, there is no direct relation between *richness* and happiness: "more income" means "more happiness", but the curve becomes horizontal after $60,000/year. Other conditions kept equal, chances are you will be happier if you earn 60K instead of 30K, but you will not be significantly happier if you make a million a year instead of the 60K (or about $12K per capita in a family of five).

"Rich Dad, Poor Dad", *"Think and Grow Rich"*.... Read those books—they are indeed interesting. But dreaming to become rich is mostly

wishful thinking and not at all necessary for individuation or for being happy. A reasonable wealth is a much more realistic goal, is attainable, and won't necessarily use up the most important resource we all (rich and poor alike) have: **time** —a non-renewable, scarce, non-purchasable (and consequently invaluable) resource.

My advice: Try to get the money you need and get all the time you *possibly can*. How? Stop spending money and time in superfluous things, of course. Focus both of them on the essential.

The only way out of inconstancy

Glory, revenge, fame, approval, richness. When all that is achieved, then what? Go wild: play the tape of your fantasies to the end. When all your enemies have bit the dust, when you are driving a Rolls Royce, when your picture is on every magazine... what would have changed, actually?

I suspect nothing would have fundamentally changed if what we do doesn't provide the meaning we were internally craving for.

It's easier said than done, but this is the general plan: 1) **choose** wisely; 2) **act** on our decisions; 3) **persist** beyond the first setbacks.

And the hardest part is point 3, because it involves two concepts us DVC's fear and hate: perseverance and discipline, both of which require character. That is something we have to grow for ourselves; no book can do that for us.

So, let's find out a mission and let's persist. Let's persist, if only because we have chosen to do so.

5

The Shadow: Cups and Cakes with The Dark Side

[ANAKIN SKYWALKER has discovered that EMPEROR PALPATINE is the Sith Lord behind the fall of the Galactic Republic. Taking advantage of ANAKIN's shaking trust on the Jedi Council, PALPATINE tries to attract him to the Dark Side of the Force. ANAKIN, with rage, ignites his lightsaber].

PALPATINE: *Are you going to kill me?*

ANAKIN: [ANGRY] *I would certainly like to!*

PALPATINE: *I know you would... I can feel your anger... It gives you focus! It makes you stronger!*

(From "Star Wars- Episode III: The Revenge of the Sith", directed by George Lucas, 2005.)

This is where typical self-help books tell people: *"You are a beautiful person, a luminous being, an unlimited blah-blah-blah"*. But since this is not a typical self-help book, I will tell you what you don't want to hear, instead.

Ok. Here we go. You are not going to like it.

A part of you exists that you don't know about. And it is dark, dirty, and even potentially deadly. So dark, dirty, and deadly that you don't even *notice* how it controls you.

But there are good news for the Da Vinci cursed. That dark, unconscious part of ourselves might hid a potential that we need to untap in order to find our life's mission.

Enter "the Shadow"

As the rest of this book will help us finding our mission by researching our passions, it is important to ask *whose* passions are we really talking about. If there are parts of our personality that are unknown to ourselves, there are, unavoidably, inclinations that we are leaving out of our analysis through denial. As if being multitalented was not enough trouble already.

You are probably familiar with this chart, called the "Johari window"; it shows the relative "size" of the different areas of our personality according to what we (and others) know about ourselves:

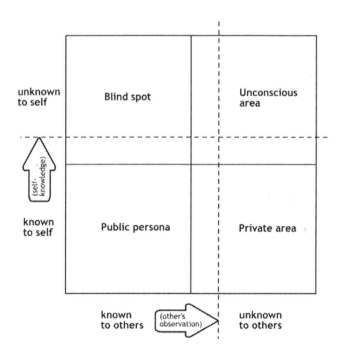

I want to discuss one aspect of the chart, represented by the vertical arrow ("self-knowledge"): The line that separates what we know from what we ignore about our own personality gets pushed further, an awareness that reduces the unconscious area via a process we can refer to as "befriending the Shadow". Note that when we learn something about ourselves, we always have the possibility of making it part of our "public persona" or keeping it safe from others' view in our "private area".

Our unconscious, which is what we will focus on in this chapter, contains all that we ignore about ourselves (things we ignore *we ignore them!)* The "Shadow" is one of the main Jungian "archetypes", which are instinctive, universal, symbolic expressions of the most basic human concepts and experiences). The Shadow, in particular, **contains all that we reject in ourselves through denial.** The things we deny are not necessarily evil things, but somewhere in our life we learned to tag them as negative, shameful, inappropriate; they are negative inasmuch they are repressed and consequently primitive. Repression does not eliminate their working capacity—it just makes it unconscious, uncontrolled, always opposing our claimed ideals and wishful efforts.[1] Our personal Shadow is also connected to a collective Shadow, the sum of neglected and repressed values of the society we are part of.

The encounter with the Shadow (the act of facing a part of us we deny) plays a central role in the process of **individuation,** integrating a fragmented, conflicting self into a functioning, stable whole.

Abraham Maslow referred to individuation (which is a Jungian term) calling it "self-actualization", defining it as:

> The desire for self-fulfillment; namely, the tendency for [the individual] to become actualized in what he is potentially. This tendency might be phrased as the desire to become more and more what one is, to become everything that one is capable of becoming.[2]

Since individuation is a task we face our whole life, and especially during the second half, it is precisely the resolution of the unconscious conflicts that allows us to become ourselves.

1: Edward C. Whitmont, The Evolution of the Shadow, in Zweig/Abrams (1991) - P. 15
2: Maslow (1943) – p. 11; Goldstein (1939) - P. 383

The Shadow's function is vital. If we didn't project our darkness outwards, we might never connect with the world at all.[3] In order to control our dark traits we must complete a cycle: deny, project, understand, and integrate.

Manifestation of our personal Shadow

But, how can we face our Shadow, if it is unconscious?

We unveil it.

The Shadow manifests itself in interesting ways:

1) **In our dreams.** Our Shadow assumes the form of particular characters in our dreams. Monsters, enemies, despised or evil characters, typically of the same gender as the dreamer. Since it represents a distant, primitive, and indiscriminate aspect of us, it is possible that it might appear with darker features, like black clothes, or a covered face. In fact, *every* character in our dreams is secretly ourselves, because a dream is a representation of our own psyche.

2) **Projected on others.** Everyone carries a Shadow, and the less it is expressed in our waking life, the blacker and denser it is.[4] The usual way to deny our Shadow (and paradoxically to reveal it, too) is by projecting it on others, and the more we deny those dark traits in ourselves, the more we project them to the outside.

The projection of the shadow is a defense mechanism. True: sometimes other people screw up, and we feel entitled to experience anger and disappointment. But many, many times **the negative we see in others is nothing more than the negative we deny in ourselves.** Since it is painful to look at that negativity in us, that blackness (just like a physical shadow) is projected *away* from us, covering others. But the source of that darkness is *us*, and denying the fact that

---

3: M. L. Von Franz, cited by Robert Bly, *The Long Bag We Drag Behind Us*, in Zweig/Abrams (1991) - p.10
4: Jung (1938) - P. 131

we project that darkness at all is a double denial. We could be alert, instead, and as soon as we detect we feel hate, anger, or other form of contempt against others (especially people of the same gender as yours), try to understand how that same thing that upsets us is present in you.

A typical example: the spouse who fears that their partner might be having an affair, even if there are no objective signs of it; or who bitterly criticizes someone else's extramarital affair. Not infrequently, the real cause of those feelings of fear and anger correspond to the accuser's *own* attraction to someone else—a situation that poses a risk to the relationship and generates stress. Consequently, it is denied in oneself but has to be placed somewhere else. Where? Outside, in the other.

Another typical example: Research shows empirical evidence that homophobia is more common and intense in people with an unacknowledged attraction to the same gender. This scientific finding is also valid for persons raised in households that forbade such desires, thus repressing such elements of the ego and rendering them unconscious.[5]

Acknowledging the presence of those repressed elements is the most important step towards individuation. By befriending the Shadow, we reverse a process that divided us in two: the person we *think* we are, and the person we *deny* we are.

See? I told you that you weren't going to like it.

Genesis of the Shadow

The repressed nature of the Shadow is imposed by society. What is more, that repressive function is the core mission of some social institutions:

- **Religion,** via the concept of "sin", the threat of damnation, and the personification of evil via the implementation of demonic fig-

---

5: Weinstein, Netta; Ryan, William S.; DeHaan, Cody R.; Przybylski, Andrew K.; Legate, Nicole; Ryan, Richard M. (2012), Parental autonomy support and discrepancies between implicit and explicit sexual identities: Dynamics of self-acceptance and defense. Journal of Personality and Social Psychology, Vol 102(4), Apr 2012 - P. 815-832.

ures; Heaven's doors smaller that the eye of a needle, which only will let the *purest* of us to pass through them; space ships with room for only 144,000 selected people, etc.

- **Pseudo-philosophies.** Self-help, New-Age, and other popular movements that delude us into thinking that we are "beings of light", thereby, denying the shadow that inevitably comes into being wherever there is light.

- **Spiritual enlightenment,** led by an industry that makes a business out of convincing us that we are one with the Universe and other grandiose, and otherwise utterly useless identifications. I have read some books that go from "you are a part of creation" to "God is everything" to "you are part of God" to "you are God, too". It sounds like the perfect recipe for psychosis.

I have tried meditation, and it works fine—but I don't necessarily want to feel that I am one with everything; I want to differentiate myself from all the rest, to understand myself and the world. Plus, that is not real Buddhist philosophy; it is a popular, misunderstood version of it—the kind of things that would make a 13th century Zen master hit you on the head with his sandal to enlighten the crap out of you and make you let go that nonsense.

The "Persona": the mask we use

The person other people see in us is a *mask*, something we present to the world to make an impression and to conceal our true nature.[6] That "person" others see is actually only a ***persona*** (a word that comes from the Latin *"per sonare"*—"made to sound", which is the function of the masks actors used in antiquity, both to increase the resonance of their voices and to *impersonate* characters). The *persona* is a much diluted version of the person *we* call "I". But it doesn't end there: what we call *"I"* is a much diluted version of the *real* us, which comprises our re-

---

6: C. G. Jung, Two Essays on Analytical Psychology (London 1953) - P. 190

pressed and forgotten selves, including denied erotic drives, hostility, aggression, and other impulses that were inconvenient and uncontrollable back then, when our psyche developed.

The anima, our contrasexual side

Our unconscious also contains the *anima* (or *"animus"* in women), an archetype that represents the feminine side in men, and the masculine side in women. We are not 100% percent men or women, in the sense that traits typically ascribed to a particular sex are also manifested in the other. Men can be intuitive, perceptive, attentive, caring, loving, and tender —all characteristics associated at a biological level with *oxytocin*, a hormone more present in women. And women can be strong, decisive, confronting, defending, and impulsive —traits associated with testosterone, a hormone segregated mainly in men. But social life, via the imposition of expected social roles tends to make us keep those contrasexual expressions repressed. For that reason, our "opposite-sex self" emerges in unconscious ways, i.e. in *dreams*.

In dreams, our contrasexual side typically manifests as a character of the opposite sex of the dreamer, usually helping us or guiding us through the difficulties of the dream.

The figure of the anima/animus is of course an integral part of our myths, represented by art and culture (see examples in the figure on the opposing page).

The *anima/animus*, as all archetypes, has a positive and a negative side, though. Dreams are compensatory, a mechanism based on those polarities: they point out what we lack in our waking life.

If we don't have enough sex, we will have erotic dreams (kindly "hosted" by our *anima/animus*); if we go to bed hungry or thirsty, we will dream of eating or drinking; if we insist in avoiding some conflict in real life, the conflict will try to call our attention by manifesting itself for example as a monster that chases us, as a way to tell us *"don't avoid me*

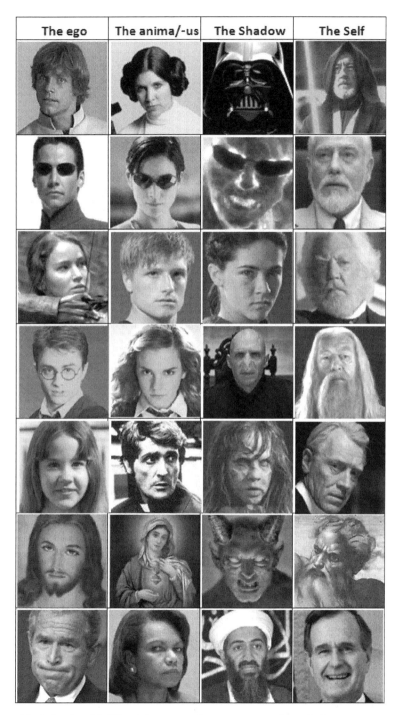

Fig. 3: Real and fictitious characters that represent archetypical structures (President Bush, Sr., is the one in the "Self" column who uses hair dye).

anymore! Deal with me!" So, the Shadow emerges in dreams. But the most concrete and "vicious" form is trough projections toward others, in waking life. For instance:

- **Toward other individuals.** Examples:
    - *"I hate that Paris Hilton; she's so stupid and superficial"*. Surely hating Paris Hilton is a clever and profound attitude to have, right?
    - *"That colleague of mine is always inviting people to her house to have sex"*. When was the last time *we* invited people to *our* house to have sex? When was the last time *we* had sex at all? Not nearly as recently as your colleague, it seems.
    - *"My neighbors are always watching what I do"*. How do we know *they* are watching *us* all the time? Because maybe *we* watch *them* all the time, that's how.
- **Towards supernatural entities**—e.g. when tragedy strikes and we find consolation by ascribing it to some unknown, superior reason ("God works in mysterious ways"). That way we hurl sadness and rage away from ourselves, which is a way of denying those perfectly normal human feelings.
- **Towards a collective.** "I hate all those stupid _____" [fill in the blank]. Examples: "fat, lazy people", "dems/reps/commies", etc.
- **From us as part of a collective** (our church, our football team, our nation) **to an individual**—usually someone with high visibility who represents *another* collective. Example: Saddam, the President, the Pope, etc.
- **From us as part of a collective, to another collective.** Individuals in power (who *deliberately* incarnate our "bright" part, our values, and our culture) exploit this resource in order to justify persecution of those "inferior" and "different", or to win elections. The most infamous example is the fascism of the Nazi years, pro-

jecting hate on several other human groups because of racial and cultural "reasons".

Now that Communism and Nazism have been rendered for the most part extinct, whom are we going to call "our enemies"? Who will serve as "the others" so that we can define ourselves in relation to that common threat? The answer is the rise of racism, homophobia, and terrorism (both real terrorism, and the kind used as an excuse to preemptively attack countries that are not on our Christmas list).

The collective Shadow is a complex matter, emergent from social dynamics and historical circumstance—a discussion that needs a clear and complete dialectical framework. Far from pretending to create a sociological treatise on the subject, I am just proposing to increase our awareness of the situations in which our Shadow manifests in us. No matter the way we project our Shadow in, an opportunity to experience a rise in self-consciousness is presented to us. All we have to do (no less) is *to observe* our identifications and understand how what we despise in others is present in us, too. Be aware of the people you despise, and then look at *which characteristic(s)* you ascribe to them you are afraid to find in yourself; look at *how* you embody that characteristic. It might not be present in you in an obvious way but in a concealed one instead (symbolic, secret, unconscious). But rest assured that if you project it away from yourself with such hate, it hides somewhere in you as well.

Denying that we possess the very characteristic we hate in the other is losing an opportunity of discovering hidden potentials, because there is no access to our unconscious but through the Shadow.

Searching for the Shadow

The person looking to discover her real self must:
- Relativize all conscious identifications. Religions, favorite teams, nation, family name… all must be understood not as *essential* but as *circumstantial*; not who we *are*, but merely what we got stuck

with. They are not personal, independent choices: they just look like that. They are merely inheritances—like money, or baldness.

- Do not (I repeat: do *not*) identify with, but *accept* the existence of that primitive, repressed, "exiled-to-the-dark" part of ourselves, the Shadow. The Shadow is not us, but merely a part of us we have to acknowledge.

I believe that leaving behind some identifications is also a way to save the energy spent holding the persona (the mask) in place. Suspending blind identifications will summon us to a kind of retirement, a temporal withdrawal from the world, a time to take our own eyes away from the usual screens.

However, there will always be a Shadow; we cannot integrate our entire unconscious (nor should we attempt to do so). But peeking into our dark side is the key to a successful individuation.

Unmasking the shadow

Some additional ideas:

- **Identify individuals or groups you despise**. We all despise Nazis, which is normal and reasonable—those bastards. But I am talking about particular people or groups that get on our nerves without much cause for it; those you would love to punch in their stupid faces, those you would love to argue with from the thinner end of a baseball bat. If your emotions get so involved, it is a sure sign of an unconscious projection. Ask yourself: In *what way* am I similar to them?

- **Receive feedback from well-intentioned people**. Friends, family and even therapists may suggest traits we have and do not accept. Those we resist the most (the ones that make us upset, or to say *"no, no, no, no"*) are probably touching a sensitive inner string. Once we accept the possibility of unconsciously having that trait in some specific, non-obvious way, though, we are in the position of looking at it with new eyes, and can try to decode its meaning.

- **Once again, pay attention to your dreams and fantasies.** Where do they wander? What do they talk about? Money, power, sexual acting out, violence, hate, desire, envy, enrichment? What's trapped inside that head of yours, clamoring for attention?

- **Resistances. Identifications.** Fascination with a person (a celebrity, for example) might indicate that we are projecting on them some quality we consider to be a positive one, an unconscious quality residing within us in a raw, potential state. Note that I am talking about *fascination* with someone, not normal admiration.

- **Humor.** Freud relates our style of humor to a particular character of our psyche: the kind of jokes we like, and especially those we make, are revealing. Observe them; jokes are not calculated—they are basically spontaneous, they stem from mental associations and as such they are a manifestation of our subconscious.

- **Slips of behavior.** When we behave in unusual ways for no clear reason (aggressively, derogatorily, sarcastically) it's a chance to become aware of the Shadow taking over our conduct.

- **Slips of the tongue.** The more embarrassing, the sexier. Err... I mean, the more interesting.

Not hunting, but befriending

This is important: when uncovering the Shadow, we must not be in "corrective" mode. We don't want to *eliminate* negative things—that way we would only push them even deeper.

Allow me to repeat the definition of Shadow, in psychological terms: it is the repressed content of our unconscious, which represents traits of our personality we do not recognize as our own. These are potentials looking for a way to shine, not to be confused with what Jung calls the "spirit-complexes"—unconscious contents that must *not* be brought up to the conscious ego and must not be associated with. Identification with these complexes, which represent grandiose structures of our collective unconscious (called the Christ-complex, the Lucifer-complex, etc.), could result in sociopathic impulses, or in psychosis. Integrating the Shadow results in a more radiant personality; integrating the spirit-complexes can result in hallucinations. I am not a psychologist, and I wouldn't dare to try to sound even remotely authoritative in these respects; obviously, in case of uncertainty regarding which part of your unconscious you are dealing with, some professional advice would be in order. *Identification* (instead of *integration*) with the Shadow is risky, too: you become a sociopath. It is a *part* of you, but it is *not* you.

Approach your Shadow with respect; befriend it. If one is to understand the Great Mystery of who we really are, one must study all its aspects, not just the dogmatic, narrow view of the conscious ego.

But remember, you are the boss.

6

Individuation:
To Be or Not To Be (You)

> [Formal hearing at Starfleet Academy. Cadet JAMES T. KIRK (Chris Pine) passed, by means of cheating, a simulated battle test designed to be unwinnable. Commander SPOCK (Zachary Quinto) inquires.]
>
> SPOCK: *Cadet Kirk, you somehow managed to activate a subroutine, thereby changing the conditions of the test.*
>
> KIRK: *Isn't the test itself a cheat? You programmed it to be unwinnable.*
>
> SPOCK: *Your argument precludes the possibility of a no-win scenario.*
>
> KIRK: *I don't believe in no-win scenarios.*
>
> SPOCK: *Then, not only did you violate the rules, you also failed to understand the principal lesson of the test. The purpose is to experience fear. Fear in the face of certain death. To accept it, and maintain control of oneself and one's crew. This is a quality expected in every Starfleet captain.*
>
> **(From "Star Trek", Directed by J. J. Abrams, 2009.)**

The midlife crisis. Have you got it yet?

By "midlife" I do not necessarily mean "age 40" or any other convention, but that inflection point in one's life that feels like a *change or die* situation, a face-to-face meeting with our existential drama.

Curiously enough, it usually happens in a moment of consolidation. Our ego (our "*self*" —small "s") has reached a critical point of integration and autonomy; as American philosopher **Ken Wilber** puts it, the person at this stage should be happy and full. But more often than not, we get profoundly unhappy. We are autonomous, and miserable:

> The world has gone flat in his appeal. No experience tastes good anymore. Nothing satisfies anymore. Nothing is worth pursuing anymore. Not because one has failed to get these rewards, but precisely because one has achieved them royally, tasted it all, and found it all lacking.
>
> The world has gone flat at exactly the moment of its greatest triumph. To whom can I sing songs of joy and exaltation? And why even should I try? It all comes to dust, yes? And where I am then?

To such conundrum, Wilber proposes leaving the "personal" behind and stepping into the "transpersonal"; a consciousness-oriented vision that I find fascinating. However, I would like to analyze this need for a change from a much less mystical standpoint.

Agreed: we are in a crisis (etymologically: a "turning point"). The call is for us to start our path of **individuation.** What is individuation? **Christopher Morley**, author of more than 100 novels, said *"There is but one success—to be able to spend your life in your own way."* I have found no better definition for it.

And the process of individuation is specially challenging for us DVC's: we like and enjoy so many things; we can't decide on one true path… How are we supposed to individuate, to find ourselves? Which road are we supposed to take, and which ones should we leave behind?

A successful individuation process has the following characteristics:

- **It has to be our own.** It requires accepting the risk of taking our own false steps instead of simply imitating others. Research shows that two-thirds of people who say they failed to achieve success in their lives point to a specific standard set by others, standards they were unable to live up to.

- **It is a process, not a single event**. Nobody wakes up one morning saying, *"Yep, from now on, I am individuated!"* It will rarely adopt the form of some sudden "enlightenment"; more often it will be a gradual development instead.

- **It is a difficult process.** Jung's view was: "You don't want to struggle? Then do not start towards individuation, because it will be all you can deal with and more".
- **It happens in the world.** It is not just some kind of *nirvana* we experience in our heads: it demands engaging reality—a place full of rules, unknown variables, and, of course, other people.
- **It is not only possible: it is also natural.** Individuation is not a therapeutic process—therapy could help, but it is first and foremost a *natural* process.

Individuation is the process of developing an integrated and healthy sense of self; in other words, it is to become the individual person we are. It happens by integrating our Shadow and by not taking our own masks (our "personas") too seriously.

The key: Endurance

Individuation is, in short, maturation. Becoming an adult. One of the tests of a psychologically mature person is to be found in her ability to handle **ambiguity**, because "black and white" stances are inevitably an incomplete view of reality. Leaning to one side or the other of a question quickly resolves the tension generated by the instability of the matter; a mature psyche, instead, can sustain the tension of opposites, thereby allowing the underlying complexity to arise.

A mature psyche can serenely wait, without taking sides, until its understanding of the subject transcends shallowness and appearances. Individuation can better take shape in an open spectrum of possibilities than in inertial personality stances.

First steps and first effects

Individuation, as an open-ended process of psychological maturity, implies gaining clarity about the person we are. It goes from the basic and general, to the specific.

The first thing we are, before anything else, is *alive*. Then we are *humans*. Then we have a gender (a biological one, but more importantly, a psychologically, self-perceived one). The first effect of an individuation "on the move" is a feeling of being better anchored in all those basic areas. We feel more alive, more human, more man or woman, *more awake*.

Find yourself first in those basic things you are and then advance on the more complex ones, the ones that evolve in time: political orientation (or lack of it), religious beliefs (or the lack of them), profession, projects, and activities.

The things you can't or won't take a position *for* or *against* (not for the moment, or ever) describe your individuality in an interesting way, too. In the end, all those decisions ("for's", "against's", and abstentions) describe the *present state* of your constantly unfolding individuation process.

Requisites for a healthy individuation

- At a functional level, it requires preservation of good mental and physical health.
- From a stability point of view, it requires resilience, the ability to bounce back from stressors and setbacks, dealing with problems as serenely and effectively as circumstances allow.
- Integration with our circumstances (social, familial, etc.), in the best way we can.
- Internalization of a more authentic idea of wellbeing, that is, defined by an inner sense of direction and accomplishment instead of external ones (social status, material goods, and third-party recognition).
- To be at peace—not ecstatic, not euphorically happy, but *at peace*—with the path we are on. Or to find a new one if we are not at peace with it.

The baggage we drag

Jung suggested that the greatest burden children must bear is the unlived life of their parents. The failed individuation of a parent is transmitted to the children in the form of either a repetition of the parents' lives or overcompensations in the opposite direction. And the unfought battles of *our* lives will be unconsciously imposed on others—especially our children, just as the unlived lives of our parents weigh on us.

Familial histories across generations reveal recurrent motifs. Genetic factors surely have a role, but more powerfully a familiar *culture* is at play—training us to make certain choices, to repeat consequences, to look at the world with a particular partiality that it is ours, too, but is fundamentally acquired. Had we been born to different parents, we would have acquired a different type of inertia, and then (as it happens now) we would hardly suspect that our perception of reality is conditioned.

As children, we learn three ways of dealing with the world:

1. We interpret emotional and tactile bonding (or its absence) as a statement about the world, directly influencing our capacity to trust others and ourselves.

2. We interpret our parents' specific behaviors as statements about *us*. As strange as it may sound, we think we *are* what our parents *act* in life, how they *treat* us.

3. We interpret *our elders' struggles* with the world as the way the world *is*. Our perception of the world is not derived from our experience (we hadn't any; we were children) but from the limited way our parents dealt with specific issues. The child cannot say "my dad has a problem". He says "the world has a problem".

As a consequence, many times we as adults do not choose, but react according to reflexes that date back to when we learned how to develop strategies for self-protection, and for little else.

But in the midlife crisis (and even before), the "Self" demands responses that transcend a simple reflex. It demands not a triggered response but a choice in resonance with something else. The person we are gets "poked" by the person we are to become. This is no new-age poetry, but an important phase of our lives, one charged with anxiety. Psychologically, it is kind of a big deal: we must "die" to be born again. It's not an end, it's a *passage*.

Baggage from adolescence. If during childhood our strategy was "to survive", during the adolescence our strategy becomes "to fit in". It is the time during which, as we insert ourselves into society, status and recognition become important for us. Looking for others' approval makes us dream of accomplishments well regarded by society. We want to become CEOs, actors, fantastic fathers and mothers, rock stars, doctors. Having replaced the magical thinking of childhood with the heroic thinking of adolescence is a good thing, though: it encourages us as we plunge into adulthood, still pursuing those same third parties', seeking-for-approval objectives. Adulthood, however, is a harder place than we thought it would be: sooner or later we realize that there is not much room at the fancy top of the social pyramid, or we realize that maybe we wanted to be somewhere else, anyway.

The middle passage

It is precisely that difference between the *expected* life and the *experienced* life that brings about the "middle passage". Magic and heroism give way to *realism*: a more down-to-earth consideration of our situation versus our aspirations. The difference is that, hopefully, this time such aspirations will be our own, not inflated by a sense of self-importance aimed at receiving approval from others.

So the midlife crisis begins: with the realization that life is not going to be what we fantasized about. But we still are either trying, using our parent's methods (repeating their lives) or doing the exact opposite, which is of course as much a conditioned behavior, as well.

The midlife crisis is, however, also an opportunity to set ourselves free, of redeeming our parents instead of being conditioned by their example, of integrating ourselves, of consolidating our personality by actualizing our potential. We are between a rock and a hard place, and one of the two will have to give.

Psychologist and author **James Hollis** puts it clearly:

> Unlike physical pain, which may be all too conscious, the pain of forced inauthenticity may remain unconscious; yet it engenders profound suffering which one may internalize as depression, externalize as violence, anaesthetize with substances, or somaticize as illness.

Midlife crises adopt the form of financial, health, and/or relationship problems; a sensation of loss of meaning—an upsetting of the day-to-day life as we were used to understand it. Something inside us wishes (and demands) an adjustment, a deep change. Midlife crises can be triggered by hard events (bereavements, financial crisis, etc.) but are fundamentally internal, even when on the outside everything looks great.

Long-term effects of individuation

No bulleted lists here. The long-term effect of a successful individuation process is (ideally) the acquisition of happiness; but more importantly, the main goal of individuation is to **provide meaningfulness** to our lives.

Let's get out of our heads and into the world. The individuation process must not be mistaken for egotism or self-absorption; paradoxically, is the other way around. Individuation is a bold intent to find out what our destiny is, and to walk bravely towards it. It means to lose the ego so we can find it; it means to embrace a larger view of ourselves, including our darker side. What have we sent into exile within us? What hides in the obscure dungeons of our souls, craving be acknowledged? Fear, anger, sadness, forgotten dreams? Facing them is not easy, but recognizing their existence will give us the focus and the strength to control them. Meaning arises even from places of great suffering, pointing the path to the life one is summoned to live.

Existentialism good for something

According to research the most common regret of those on their deathbeds is something along the lines of: *"I wish I'd had the courage to live a life true to myself, not the life others expected of me."*

As Jung said, death cannot be avoided: it can only be outgrown. May our deathbed regrets be few and whimsical; a sign that the important things got taken care of. Alright, alright: we cannot cheat death, and existence is cruel. I agree. However, the invitation here is to leave that rejoicing in desperation behind, and cultivate a new kind of existentialism; one that actually accomplishes something. Life isn't a no-win scenario. We can win by achieving the one success of us mortals: individuation. An such an important step is usually marked by rites of passage. Are you ready to take the next step?

7

Rites Of Passage: Stepping Into a New World

> [JACK (Edward Norton) sits on the toilet, cordless phone to his ear, and flips through an IKEA catalog. There's a stack of old *Playboy* magazines and other catalogs nearby.]
>
> JACK: [VOICE OVER] "Like everyone else, I had become a slave to the IKEA nesting instinct."
>
> JACK: [INTO PHONE] *Yes. I'd like to order the 'Erika Pekkari' slip covers.*
>
> JACK: [VOICE OVER, WHILE WAITING FOR THE ANSWER OF THE IKEA SALESPERSON] "I would flip through catalogs and wonder, 'What kind of dining set defines me as a person?' We used to read pornography. Now it's the 'Horchow' Collection."
>
> **From "Fight Club", directed by David Fincher, 1999.**

A few days after I successfully took my last test at the university I was walking by a small square in my hometown; suddenly, for some reason unclear to me at the moment, I had to stop and sit on a bench: a deep sadness invaded me; a profound sense of loss, instead of the expected sense of accomplishment I should have at the end of my university years. And I had no clue why. I made a heroic effort to contain my tears, barely successful.

It was only after a few days that I understood what was going on: my "birth" as a professional implied the "death" of what I was before. The sadness I felt was the mourning of my student-self, and also fear of the incoming challenges.

The symbolic death/re-birth event is the essence of all personal transitions; however, important transitions in our lives often do not receive their due recognition, from society or from us. They go by unnoticed, without the chance of symbolically snapping in place in our minds.

When I talk about "symbolic events" it must not be assumed that they are less important or less real than "real" events. There are only *events*, the "symbolic" being their internal dimension, and "real" being the occasion—the external, social side (wedding, baptism, etc.).

In the next chapters we will work on our portfolio of activities. An external change in our lives will be made, changes which have an *external* dimension (activities, timelines, agendas, etc.) but also an *internal* change will happen, one that might represent a point of inflection in our lives. Points of inflection must not go unnoticed; they need a conscious, *explicit* acknowledgement; such is the role of the **rites of passage**.

These ritual steps, their sequence, structure, and motifs are similar among the most diverse human cultures, separated by such great distances in time and space that it is impossible that they were simply transmitted by tradition; there are no "central committees" for these things: making an analogy with computers, we may say that it is recorded in humanity's *firmware*.

The function of rituals

Rituals have a channeling function: they direct the flow of our *libido* (our primal energies) in meaningful ways. I am convinced that rituals are actions whose intention is to control the future, too. They have a magical nature, but, fundamentally, they have an existential one. The future is the place where death awaits for everyone, and by acting out myths, humans seek to attract and ensure the most basic object of desire: life.

Any consideration of rituals has necessarily a mythic tone. Note that I didn't say "mystic", "religious", or "theological", but *mythic*. Whatever our spiritual beliefs may be, we are bound to *myths* because our psyche is structured around them; their images are the most basic conceptualizations of the world, consequences of our experience with the world since time immemorial.

That is one positive function of religion: to act as a resource to project our pathological grandiosity outside of the human realm. Myth (religious myth in particular) has the numinous function of remitting our "god-energies" somewhere else—to a god that can deal with them, because we can't. Even if one may not believe in all that theologically, it is true psychologically.

That redirection is necessary to unburden our mind from the narcissistic impulse of being the center of the universe—an understandable temptation since we perceive the world from here and towards our surroundings: from our standpoint, the universe is a sphere made of everything else with us at the center.

In ancient times (and even today in many parts of the world) anchoring the human realm to a transcendent realm provided stability to social structures, making them strong enough to withstand the disintegrating forces of time: change and decay. So, rituals are an invocation to myth, connecting the day-to-day to the transcendental.

Rituals have not so much religious but fundamentally *pagan* roots (paganism being a sort of a proto-religion addressing natural forces). I believe that rituals should be particularly important for non-religious persons. In a religion, the narcissistic transference to a god is made via prayer or meditation. For a non-religious person, ideally, a time comes when the balloon that we are is not so full of narcissistic gas, so *no* flattening ballasts (depression and shame—discussed in chapter 13) are necessary to prevent it from going astray (psychosis), and it is finally free to find its own, realistic ceiling.

The missing rites in modern life

Imagine that after a very romantic proposal, you find yourself engaged to the person you always dreamt of. Then imagine that, automatically, right there and from then on, you two are *married*. Just like that.

Something doesn't feel right, does it? Something is missing. If the ritual is absent, it is as if the marriage didn't happen at all. Such an important event *has* to be acknowledged and experienced in the multiple dimensions in which humans operate:

- External orders: in the social, legal, familial. The accent on each area is provided by the priest (or judge), the ceremony, the party, family, friends and the different roles they play, the honeymoon, the bride's dress, the official records, the cake, the video, the rings, and many other things.

- Internal orders: rituals are the most basic activity that address *all* human dimensions: they connect the three orders of human experience—the real, the symbolic, and the imaginary. Rituals and rites of passage are life events (real order) anchored to myths (imaginary order) rooted in the unconscious (symbolic order).

Note that unimportant, routine events are sometimes called "a ritual", but only because of their repetitive character, not because of their symbolic importance. We hire a DJ to musicalize our wedding, but not our morning's tooth brushing, which is not actually a ritual, but a habit.

The one passage that interests us the most right now is the passage into **adulthood**. Legally recognized in terms of a numeric value (18, 21, or some other number of years), adulthood is blurry in terms of an internal transformation of the person from child to man or woman.

Ask some friends in their forties to close their eyes and make their minds blank for a few seconds. Then ask them how old they are according to how they *feel*. We feel as if we were still 20, 25, or whatever (relatively small) number represents that internal sense of age.

Other version of the question is (answer spontaneously): *"To what 'percentage' do you feel like an adult person?"* I cannot avoid but say something like 75%. We have an inner sense of maturity, but we also may feel as if our adulthood has not reached critical mass, like we cannot say that we feel "a hundred percent" adults. And why should that be otherwise? When does adulthood become evident? It is like the frog in a pot full of water that's getting imperceptibly hotter and hotter. When is it *critically* hot? When *precisely* do I become an adult?

I can act as an adult, but adulthood is not only happening externally; in order to become an adult *internally* (to my own perception) a special event—a rite of passage—is needed to mark it.

Jews have *Bar-* and *Bat-Mitzvah's*; not that 13 year old boys and girls are ready to feel one hundred percent adults right there and then, but it's at least something. Are Mitzvah's enough—or even *timely*? What happens with other cultures in which no such rites exist?

Consequences of losing rituals

The first consequence for men, in particular, is that we doubt our masculinity. What is more, the stupid things male adolescents get involved in (vandalism, risky motorcycle tricks, hazing) are a way to prove themselves, a desperate try to show the world that they are men. Girls have their own equivalents: the search for approval through popularity is an example. But girls have a fundamental, biological advantage: their first period and all the physical, reproductive, and privacy-related implications that come with it. Also, they have *maternity*: giving birth can be a transformative experience. Boys don't have periods or labor—when we are adolescents we have fireworks and graffiti, or worst things yet, like drugs or motorcycle tricks.

The problem is that missing conscious rituals get replaced by unconscious ones: addictions. Substance abuse, sexual addiction, gambling and compulsive shopping (at IKEA or otherwise) can be understood as pseudo-rituals that people use to regulate those undirected grandiose energies.

Addictions are the manifestation of a grandiose ego to which an escape valve has been denied to; not intense enough to borderline with psychosis but capable of creating significant symptoms, nonetheless.

Is there a way out? Surely. Apart from therapy, possibilities on a personal level are not scarce. We can cultivate positive personal rituals. We have identified two types of ritual: the day-to-day ones (habits), and the "special-occasion" ones. Regarding rituals understood as habits, physical exercise is the best of the best. Getting "addicted" to exercising 3 to 5 times per week has been proven to be exceedingly beneficial to our overall health and for prolonging life. Let your exercise program be a conscious ritual, a sort of liturgy that marks a "sacred" space and time. The religious metaphor is deliberate; it is precisely such a "devotional" attitude that confers the meaning we are missing elsewhere, changing unconscious, unproductive, addiction-driven pseudo rituals to conscious, controlled, and beneficial rituals. Also, physical exercise has some immediate, short-term benefits as well: a sense of accomplishment, contact with nature (its colors, smells, spaces) and the segregation of endorphins, self-produced *morphine-like* chemicals that combat pain and stress.

Regarding rituals as "rites of passage", we need something else. We need to travel our own "path of the hero".

The phases of ritual

Joseph Campbell and other observers of the social and anthropological scene agree that our culture has lost the "mythic roadmap" which helps locate humans in a larger, transcendental context.

The only "transcendental" dominion in modern life is approached by religion; for those not subscribing to any faith, that role is sometimes approached by meditation. But it is not enough; sacraments and meditation sessions are not necessarily aligned with the transformations we need on a personal, individual level.

Virtually all ancient cultures had rites of passage: highly symbolic ones to which great importance was given. The most terrible initiation rite I have heard of is the *Satere-Mawe* warrior rite. To become a warrior, the boys in this Brazilian tribe stick one hand in a container made of big leaves, full of the so called "bullet" ants. The name of the insect is inspired by their sting, which is said to be as painful as a gunshot. It is described as causing "waves of burning, throbbing, all-consuming pain that continues unabated for up to 24 hours". In fact, the bullet-ant sting is ranked as the most painful by the Schmidt Sting index, some kind of terrifying scientific indicator that I didn't even have the courage to google up.

To fully complete the initiation, however, the boys must go through the ordeal *twenty times* over the course of several months or even years. Such a practice represents the other extreme of the spectrum of rites, one that goes from agonizing ceremonies in one hand (pun intended), or no rites at all on the other.

Are rites of passage that important, really?

We humans are highly symbolical beings. Our understanding of the world and of each other is based on language; even our psyche itself is structured as a language, in particular our unconscious. So, the lack of rites means that our passages are experienced in frightening and isolated ways, for there is little help from peers who are equally adrift, or from elders who already went through the same.

Despite cultural, geographical, and historical differences, traditional rites of passage typically involve six stages. These steps are:

1. Separation from the parents (often through a ritual sort of "kidnapping").
2. Symbolic "death" of the child: The tie with the parents has to be broken in order for the young to become an adult.
3. Rebirth; a "new person" steps into life.

4. The teachings: the initiated is told the primal myths, responsibilities, and knowledge (about hunting, child bearing, etc.) necessary for adult functioning.

5. The ordeal, normally in the form of a challenge that implies a further separation so the youth can find the strength within and consolidate his stance in the face of adversity.

6. The return, whereby one reenters the community with the resources in place to play a mature role. Often the initiated is given a new name to befit the radical transformation.

These steps are of course also reflected in myths and stories of a society, for example:

- In works of fiction. Myriad stories and narratives (including Harry Potter, the Matrix, Star Wars, and a never-ending list of others) from all times and cultures, reveal the steps detailed above.

- In real, social processes. College, for example: you get "isolated" from your family, you receive teachings, you prove yourself via tests and a final ordeal (a thesis), and then you reenter society with your name changed: you are now called a "doctor", "lieutenant", or something else. Military service, pilgrimages, and other instances have a similar structure and function.

The question is: "What happened with *my* hero's journey?" My suspicion is that, if it never happened to us, then it lies ahead. For those who "suffered" going through college, military service, a migration (or some other "marking" event), separation from home may have served as a sort of rite of passage into adulthood. Others were not that fortunate.

Without traditional rites of passage, adolescents identify themselves with pop culture, urban tribes, peer groups, and teen celebrities; that is, referents in their same age group who incarnate some meaning. Not that such meaning is profound, of course: it is just strong enough as to provide a name, a social recognition, some identity. The celebrity role models, through success, have defeated anonymity, insignificance and confusion. The problem is that the model does not always incarnate virtue: drugs, leaked sex-tapes, driving-under-the-influence, rehabs, probations, 72-day-long marriages, and attention-begging eccentricities dominate the personality of such role models.

Absent, unconscious, and ineffective rituals do not fulfill their central mission, which is to outgrow our childish, narcissistic self. No matter how old we are, the whimsical, spoiled, self-entitled child that we all carry inside must give way to something else—our true *self*.

What do you say? Shall we start looking for it?

PART II

(Where we consider many
potential activities, filter them,
and decide our mission in life.)

8

Inventory of Dreams

[PETER GIBSON (Ron Livingston) a cool, young man with a terrible job at Initech (a company that incarnates all that's wrong with corporations) talks with his redneck neighbor LAWRENCE (Diedrich Bader), who works in the demolition business]

[PETER]   Lawrence, what would you do if you had a million dollars?

[LAWRENCE]   I'll tell you, man: Two chicks at the same time. Now, what would you do?

[PETER]   If I had a million dollars? *Nothing. I would relax, I would sit on my ass all day. I would do... nothing.*

[LAWRENCE]   *You don't need a million dollars to do nothing, man. Take a look at my cousin. He's broke, he don't do shit.*

(From "Office Space" — Directed by Mike Judge, 1999.)

The objective of the next few chapters is to build our new portfolio of activities. It starts now and ends in chapter 11.

Let me start with a word of caution: Preparing the portfolio (that is, going through the next 4 or 5 chapters) will take you a few hours; implementing it is a whole different game that will require patience, carefulness, and intelligence—the work of months.

Also, this is an *iterative* process, not a linear one. As you get more understanding of the activities you may do and the reasons behind such inclinations, it will be necessary to go back and rethink some decisions. The more repetitive this process is on paper, the more straightforward will it be in real life.

These are the next steps we will follow:

1. **We will create an <u>inventory</u> of dreams** and understand the ambitions and intentions that drive them. At which level of proficiency and to what ends would we want to perform that/those activities? (This chapter).

2. **We will <u>rank</u> the candidate activities.** We will measure those dreams against our talents and the realistic chances of making money with them (chapters 9 and 10).

3. **We will create a life <u>portfolio</u>,** qualifying the activities that made it through the previous filters (chapters 11 and 12).

Download the Excel Spreadsheet!

I have created a small Excel spreadsheet that you can download from bit.ly/dvcurse. It will make the process detailed in the next pages easy a breeze, and it will build your portfolio automatically.

A	B	C	D	E	F	G
	INVENTORY OF DREAMS	Wish	Talent	Money	Composed	RESULTS
1	Learning to play harpsichord					
2	Playing tennis					
3	Obtaining my license as masseur					
4	Start my own business (used books store)					
5	Start my own business (vintage bike parts)					
6	Learning to draw portraits					
7	Finish my novel and submit it to a wrinting contest					
8	Current job: customer sat supervisor at Initech					
9	Current side Job: building handmade pipes					
10	Current hobby 1: Bycicle riding twice a week					
11	Current hoby 2: building airplane models					

So, here we go.

First step: The inventory of dreams

Make a list of everything you would like to do. *Ev-ree-thing*.

Use your wishes as the main parameter, taken as independently as you can from other considerations. It doesn't matter (yet) if you have the talent or not. It doesn't matter (yet) if you can make money from it. Consider this a "brainstorm" session: every crazy idea is valid. If you'd like to do it, just put it on the list. It is important to be as exhaustive as you can. I don't want you to reach the end of this book and say *"Parasailing! Oh, I forgot parasailing!"* (or teaching yoga, or whatever).

Also include in the list:

- All the **jobs** you would like to have (examples: to be a professional chess player, to open a florist business, to be a guitar professor).
- All the **hobbies** you would like to have (example: learn to play competitive chess, learn how to make ikebana flower arrangements, learn to play guitar).
- All the **one-time** activities you would like to do (example: to play in a chess tournament just for fun, make a flower arrangement for your anniversary dinner next month, learn to play a couple of Beatles songs on the guitar).

Note that I have chosen different degrees of involvement for the **same three activities**: chess, flower arrangement, guitar. It doesn't matter if you are duplicating activities by listing them as "desired jobs" and "desired hobbies" simultaneously: simply go ahead. It is not even necessary to categorize them as jobs, hobbies, or one-time-things: in fact, it is better if you don't.

Deliberately ignore all money-related considerations. Imagine that you would have all the money you would need to carry on a normal life, with all basic needs well covered.

Imagine age is not a problem, either. Gender, physical constitution... nothing should matter —for now. Did you always want to be a jockey (riding race horses) but you are 6 foot tall and weigh 250 lbs? Write *"To be a jockey"* in that list, nonetheless. What we want is to list, once and for all, the complete palette of activities that appeal to you; we want to take everything that is out there and pass it through the filter of your interests and inclinations. That is why more down-to-earth parameters (monetization and talents) are put on-hold for now.

Important: Each item should have the form *"verb + activity"* and be as short and precise as possible. Your list might include, for example:

- Learning how to play an instrument (what instrument?) Example: "Learn guitar"
- Playing a sport (which sport?) - Example: "To become a competitive basketball player"
- Studying a foreign language (which one?) - Example: "Learn Japanese"
- Getting a diploma (on what?) - Example: "Get a chemistry degree"
- Writing a book (about what?) - Example: "Write a cook book"
- "Traveling to Mongolia" (or wherever works for you).
- "Parachute jumping" (this one is nowhere near my own list).

Now, include things you think you have talent for. It doesn't matter whether you have tried those particular activities or not. If you think you could be good at something (even if you are not too excited about trying) *include it.*

If you ever cooked a wonderful meal and someone at the table said *"Oh, this is delicious! You should become a professional cook"* then add "to become a cook" in your inventory of dreams, too.

What do you think you could get paid to do? Maybe you learned some things (baking cakes, repairing bikes, whatever). Include them in the list.

Make a mental list of people you admire and would like to emulate. Painters, physicists, photographers, poets, politicians, pianists, porn stars. Then include those professions in your dreams' inventory, too. (Not that you would like to be an adult-movie luminary—would you?)

Include things you are too old for. Include "being an astronaut" if you ever dreamed about that. You know that such activity is highly unlikely to get to the finals of your decision. The point of including all these activities is to reach a sense of *closure* for most of them; instead of having them hanging somewhere as "unfulfilled pendings", you will drain them out of your agenda by conscious decision. By including them in your wish list, you will either *do* them, or discard them. They get resolved, in one way or the other.

Now, this is crucial:

Include in your list all the activities you are engaged in right now:

- **Your current job** (especially if you **don't** like it. Bad dreams are dreams, too).
- **Old jobs** you fondly remember.
- **Side jobs** (any activity that puts some occasional extra money on your wallet).
- **Current hobbies,** and past hobbies that you enjoyed.

You should have at least 30 or 40 items in your list. If not, keep thinking. An "average" case of DVC should have over 50 items. Ideally, you can list 70 or more activities –that should be enough even for a serious case of the da Vinci Curse.

Why is it so important to be exhaustive? Because (although it is far from evident yet) we have to make sure that activities with the potential to be combined to form the mission of our lives have been included. The more things you want to include, the better; this exercise is not a question of minutes: it should take hours, or even a few days. Take your time.

Your list should look like this (note that the columns on the right are empty—filling them up comes later on, that's what these couple of chapters are about):

"To be" dreams vs. "to have" dreams

Note carefully that all dreams I am asking you to list imply action, not materialistic aspirations. You want a new car? Good for you—I don't care. When you get a new car, you do not get *transformed* in anything different (except into a debtor, perhaps). Now, traveling to Mongolia or getting a degree in accountancy... well, that's different—you *become* a travelled person or an accountant. Or so it seems at first sight.

In his classic book *To Have or To Be,* **Erich Fromm** tells us about how each human experience can occur in one of those two modes. One thing is becoming an accountant, and the other is just having a diploma that says so. *Experiencing* an exotic adventure in Mongolia (its culture, history, cuisine, and traditions) is not the same as accumulating miles, buying crappy memorabilia, and getting your friends' admiration by showing them the pictures you took.

If you want to keep a separate list of "to have" dreams (things to buy, awards to win, people to seduce, salary raises to get) by all means do so. We will not need it.

Small dreams, big dreams

At this point, it doesn't matter much if the activities on your list are defined as something bigger (or smaller) than your real talents can encompass. In the next chapters, we will instill some realism into them. However, it helps if you can make your dreams somewhat realistic.

Let's say you have a strong interest in astronomy. One too big dream would be *"to discover a new extra-solar planet, which from then on will be known as the* '[insert your name here] *planet'"*. That is not only unrealistic (planets are discovered by specialized people strongly funded, with access to incredibly powerful equipment) but it is also a dream that is ego-centered and narcissistic. On the other hand, if you describe your astronomy-related aspirations as simply "read Stephen Hawking's last book", it may not make justice to your interest on the subject. A realistic, reasonable dream would be "to learn astronomy", which will imply taking some courses and having access to a telescope (maybe at your local observatory, or on eBay: for less than 250 bucks you find nice, well used computerized telescopes—I just checked). If the dream is to learn astronomy, plan to start looking *up:* that's realistic enough. And the same goes for the rest of your activities.

Remember, we are talking *activities* here, not "pendings". Activities are things that have continuity in time, things at which we become better, things we could eventually monetize. Pendings are tasks, to-dos, events to be placed in an agenda, things that need a date and a time (discussed in chapter 13). If something has a learning curve, it is an activity; if it has a deadline, it is a pending.

1. How badly do I want to do this?

Once you have finished your inventory of dreams, qualify them according to the following scale (simply write the corresponding number on the column "Wish" in your spreadsheet):

1	"I don't really care *that* much about this; would be fun to try."
2	"It would be nice to do it; it could be interesting indeed."
3	"I have to give it a try; it has intrigued me for a long time now."
4	"I *must* do it. I always wanted to, I have to do it."

2. The talent score

We DVC's are addicted to having our minds blown. We love to discover facts and ideas that bend and expand our minds.

Continuing with the "astronomy" example, the following is an idea that blew my mind recently: Scientists in Spain are working on the premise that the universe is not expanding, really, but it is *time* itself that is gradually slowing down. A point will arrive (billions upon billions of years from now) in which time might not flow anymore, and everything will remain immobile "forever" (a word without meaning in a universe with no time.)

What can be more tempting for a DVC than cosmology? We love big pictures, and the universe itself is the biggest of them all. Investigating the subject further, though, I looked at some papers on the subject. See if you can make sense of this:[7]

> For simplicity we will only consider branes Σ spherical, plane or hyperboloidal symmetry, i.e. a metry-preserving matching [7]. Then, ignoring tl gular coordinates, the corresponding hypersurfac given in parametric form by $\Sigma : \{t = t(\xi), r = r(\xi)\}$ $\tilde{\Sigma} : \{\tilde{t} = \tilde{t}(\xi), \tilde{r} = \tilde{r}(\xi)\}$. The matching implies [3 the first fundamental form on the brane reads
>
> $$ds^2|_\Sigma = N(\xi)d\xi^2 + a^2(\xi)d\Omega_k^2$$
>
> where $a(\xi)$ is defined by $r(\xi) = \tilde{r}(\xi) = a(\xi)$ and controls the embedding functions $t(\xi)$ and $\tilde{t}(\xi)$ via
>
> $$\dot{t} = \frac{\sigma a}{k + \lambda^2 a^2}\sqrt{\frac{\dot{a}^2}{a^2} - N\left(\frac{k}{a^2} + \lambda^2\right)}$$

Note that the paragraph starts with the words *"For simplicity"*. And that was only page 1 of the paper. Imagine what kind of hell awaits in the following ones. I am an engineer; I am no stranger to math. But after 15 minutes investigating the subject, I decided that cosmology would only make a nice hobby for me—maybe reading a book about it now and then, but that was all.

Such is the kind of analysis each activity in your wish list has to be submitted to. Then, rate them according to how well each activity matches your *current* talents:

7: Mars, M.; Senovilla, J.; Vera, R. (2007), Is the accelerated expansion evidence of a forthcoming change of signature on the brane? - ArXiv.org > gr-qc > arXiv:0710.0820v2.

1	"**I am not at all suited for this,** even if it would be fun to try. My age / health / training / lack of professional license, or some other deal-breaking factor make this activity impossible to be taken seriously by me."
2	"**I might succeed,** if I put a lot of effort, time and training. It will take me a minimum of 3 to 5 years to obtain the necessary education and permits necessary to work in this activity"
3	"**I could get really good at this;** I have the talent and knowledge required. I have formal education / training in this area, and I have a clear idea of the steps I must follow."
4	"**I was born to do this.** I could be one of the best in the field."

In order to correctly evaluate your talents for each activity, please take also the following parameters into account (as you can see, now we start to combine *dreams* with *realism*):

Health. This is possibly the first consideration. There is no point in pursuing activities that could worsen a health condition; however, for many people, health can be a reason to increase some activities' scores. If you are overweight, for example, you can only benefit by increasing your physical activity, even if you are not going after an Olympic medal.

Age. Trying to become a world-class athlete, dancer, or concertist when pushing 50 is not going to work well; having fun at sports, dancing, or playing music at 50 is perfectly possible, though, provided that some minimal physical conditions are present. The activities are the same; what changes is the scope of potential in relation to your age. Let the "talent scores" for each activity reflect that, too.

Formal training. For each activity, ask the following: *What is your present training level? What would take to put you on the next level?* Some activities require formal training and licensing. One can spend decades studying alone to become a self-made entomologist, but without holding a PhD or at least a degree in biology the chances of being taken seriously are non-existent. If you are 18, you might have no excuse to avoid biology school; if you are 48, you might want to careful ponder the cost/benefit ratio of taking up things that require an academic degree of involvement.

By the way: did you know that many plumbers make more money than PhD's? A study by *The Economist* says the following:

- Many PhD students describe their work as "slave labor".
- The number of PhD positions has no relation to the number of job openings.
- A PhD may offer no financial benefit over a master's degree. It can even reduce earnings.
- The fiercest critics compare research doctorates to "Ponzi" schemes. Education is vital. But it doesn't *necessarily* have to be the highest academic level available: it needs to be accurate, complete, and relevant to our intentions. But of course, an excess of education rarely killed anyone—lack of education surely did.

Learning curve. What is the learning curve each activity requires to provide a return in performance or satisfaction? For example, learning to play at a good level on a "stick" (a beautifully minimalist musical instrument) takes months, if not years; the same goes for the violin and the oboe. But on a guitar you could be playing simple songs within a couple of weeks. Weigh in the learning curves.

How good do you intend to become at it? For each activity in your portfolio, you should understand what level of proficiency you intend to reach.

Imagine I want to learn how to play the piano. I do play some guitar; I certainly have an ear for music, and I can read it a little. But I am a total newbie regarding the piano. At this point I am an outsider, I cannot play piano, I would need to learn, to train, and to study. But playing piano is not the only thing I want to do—I am a DVC. I want to do lots of things. And as described at the beginning of the book, there is a trade-off between the number of activities in my portfolio and the level of proficiency I could reach on each of them. The following figure shows that trade-off.

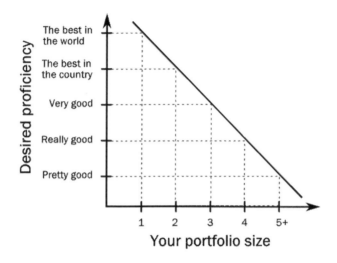

Figure 5: How good you can reasonably become at things, depending on how many of them you do at the same time.

Note that the chart is optimistic: I haven't heard of anyone who is "the best in the country" at two different things simultaneously. I don't even know of anyone who is "pretty good" at *five* different things at the same time, as the chart shows.

Evaluating your talents as honestly as possible will save you the pain of falling back under the power of our da Vinci curse: starting things and abandoning them too soon. Don't just say, *"I want to be the best in the world!"* after reading a Dale Carnegie book. Maybe you do *not* want that. Being the best at something demands no less than complete dedication, leaving no time for a diversified portfolio.

What is the level you want to reach with each activity? What is there, apart from being "the best in the world"? Well, you can be:

- **A private amateur**. The word "amateur" is sometimes used in a derogatory sense. That is sad and inaccurate, since it comes from the Latin *amator*, lover. An amateur is someone fascinated by a particular subject, enjoying the freedom of not having to make money from it. An amateur happily hunts for information in books, on the web, and in other sources; she is accountable only to herself, and she can leave the activity anytime, or stop doing it for months or years, and start again as if no time has passed. Fame or fortune is not to be expected, though; as the word's etymology reminds it, an amateur does it for the love of it.

- **A serious amateur**, someone with a deeper involvement in terms of money and time. That activity is an occasion for social interaction, camaraderie, recreational competition, traveling, attending conventions, and reading (deciphering) more specialized material.

- **A Semi-pro,** someone who has found a practical form of monetizing an activity on a part-time basis, possibly using third party services (e.g. eBay, Elance, etc.). It is normally an independent activity (you are your own boss), complementing a day job in order to have more financial stability. Examples: you make some money on the side by playing the sax in a jazz band; you create some product at home and sell it online, etc.

- **A Full-time professional,** one that makes a life out of an activity, working several hours per day, 5-6 days a week / 48-50 weeks a year, competing with others already established in the same trade. It involves an increased accountability: a more strict compliance with laws, balance books, management of human resources, bank loans, business tax declarations, etc. Your stakeholders are not only you, but also your family, employees, partners, and customers.

- **A researcher on the subject**, someone whose work pushes the boundaries of a discipline. Think scientific method, painstaking experiments, elaboration of detailed documentation, producing original papers for peer-review, doing fundraising, competing for grants. It includes the responsibilities of a professional, a relatively less stable financial security, and a more isolated lifestyle: not many people would understand what you do.

Rate each activity as objectively as possible. Our enthusiasm may make us think that we are ready to go all the way. We want to be the best in the world, and there is no stopping us. We might have read a lot of self-help books that tricked us into believing that the universe is conspiring to make all wishes come true, but that is just written chicken soup for the soul. If you are going to do this, you have to get real, not mystical. This is a path that ultimately will make your soul feel *authentically* well, but only after achieving longer term accomplishments.
So, after evaluating each activity in such way, write the corresponding talent score in a new column:

A	B		C	D	E	F	G
	INVENTORY OF DREAMS		Wish	Talent	Money	Composed	**RESULTS**
	1	Learning to play harpsichord	2	3			
	2	Playing tennis	2	2			
	3	Obtaining my license as masseur	2	3			
	4	Start my own business (used books store)	4	4			
	5	Start my own business (vintage bike parts)	3	1			
	6	Learning to draw portraits	4	4			
	7	Finish my novel and submit it to a wrinting contest	3	2			
	8	Current job: customer sat supervisor at Initech	4	4			
	9	Current side job: building handmade pipes	3	3			
	10	Current hobby 1: Bycicle riding twice a week	3	2			
	11	Current hobby 2: building airplane models	2	2			

3. Chances of monetization

A third parameter has to be rated: the chance you think you have of making money with each activity in your list.

1	"I have no interest or chance to make money with this; there is either a highly competitive market, or I just want to pursue this as a hobby. In fact, doing this will not put any money in my pocket, but will probably take money away from it."

2	**"Monetizing this would be very difficult.** This needs big investments, a lot of expertise, and special training. There are no guarantees of making money anytime soon, or of succeeding at all in this endeavor, really."
3	**"I could make money out of this.** I know the market, I have access to this activity's community, or I could re-convert my present business or profession easily. With a minimal investment of money and time I could have the required infrastructure in place (systems, location, distribution, etc.)"
4	**"I am ready to make money with this.** I could easily transition into this activity; I have the time, the know-how, and there is an unsatisfied demand for this. I could easily get all permits / licenses and all else I need to start selling this product / service in the short term."

Nobody has a magic crystal ball; we are talking estimations here, so rate each activity in your list as realistically as you can.

If building an independent business is the way you have decided to go, a more precise evaluation is unavoidable: a real *business plan*. Elaborating a business plan lies beyond the scope of this book, but know that a business plan is an invaluable tool in deciding if the business you have in mind is viable at all, how to start it, and how to make it succeed. Right now, though, to better choose among the 4 possible ratings, consider the following issues for each activity:

- **The local market.** Where are you located? Are you able/planning to move to some other place? If your potential project is to open a frozen-yogurt place in Anchorage, Alaska, maybe considering some alternative, southern city (something like "Miami" kind of southern) could be a good idea.

- **The potential customers.** Do you know who they are? Are you already participating in the community of people that consumes the product or service you plan to sell?

- **The competitors.** Whose business are you about to compete with? It is one thing going against your old, local book store by offering better services and products, but quite another going online to build a website that challenges Amazon.com.

- **The barriers to entry.** Any intent of establishing a new Internet browser as the global default is doomed: a company and a product like Google cannot be beaten, not even by companies of comparable size with decades of experience (examples: Yahoo and Bing). But (continuing with this example) if you happen to be in the computer industry, the market is always keen for new computer games. The market is dominated by top level competitors—extremely creative, experienced, and constantly developing paradigm-setting technologies. But if your product is good enough, it *could* elbow itself in. This is an over-simplified example: the point is to understand that different businesses and positions have different barriers of entry. Some are easier to jump, others are impossible—your scoring should factor that in, too.

- **Your marketing strength.** Experience, location, and size of staff are important, but no other aspect of running a small business is as predictive of success as the level of resources it dedicates to marketing. And there is something not very fair when it comes to marketing: the biggest contender (the one with more money and advertising firepower) almost always wins.
  Moral: be careful for what niche you are going to fight, and against whom.

Welcome to wherever you are

So, at this point you have all your dreams on an Excel sheet, and each dream has three numbers associated. That causes the Excel sheet to label each activity according to their rightful quality (**Opportunities, Garbage**, and so on. Full details in the next pages).

At least 80% of the activities on your list are either going to be discarded or will only deserve a minimal investment of time and energy. But a few of them (hopefully one or two; maybe three, tops) will be the genesis of what we were looking for. That's right: in the next chapter we will take all those little dreams of yours and we will go *Pareto* on their butts.

Welcome to wherever you are. Keep going, knowing that we are onto something important here: we are preventing our souls from being haunted by the ghosts of dreams past.

9
Wishes vs. Talents vs. Money

[Nighttime. HARRY POTTER (Daniel Radcliffe), RON (Rupert Grint) and HERMIONE (Emma Watson) must leave the dorms to prevent the Philosopher's Stone from being stolen. They stop walking when they hear croaking: NEVILLE LONGBOTTOM'S (Matthew Lewis) pet toad has given the alarm]

[RON] *Trevor, shh! Go away, you shouldn't be here!*

[NEVILLE] [APPEARING FROM BEHIND A CHAIR] *Neither should you. You're sneaking out again, aren't you?*

[HARRY] *Neville, listen...*

[NEVILLE] *No! I won't let you! You'll get Gryffindor in trouble again! I'll fight you!* [HOLDS OUT FISTS]

[HERMIONE] *Neville, I'm really, really sorry about this...*

[SHE TAKES OUT HER WAND AND SAYS]

"Petrificus Totalus"!!

[NEVILLE GETS FROZEN AND FALLS BACKWARDS ONTO THE GROUND, COMPLETELY IMMOBILIZED]

[RON] [TO NEVILLE] *It's for your own good, you know.*

(From "Harry Potter and the Philosopher's Stone" - Directed by Chris Columbus, 2001.)

By **ranking our dreams** by wish, talent, and monetization we have categorized them according to the logic described on the next figure:

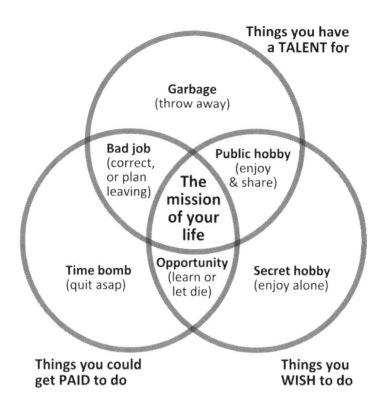

All your wishes can now be understood as pertaining to one of the following categories:

"Garbage"

I always had the strange sensation that I had a talent for golf. I don't know why; I just knew it—not that I was much interested in becoming a golfer, though. Finally, at 32, I decided to take a lesson. The golf teacher asked me several times, especially after seeing me hit 170+ yard strokes: *"You say this is the first time you grabbed a golf club"? You're kidding me, right?"* I wasn't.

Maybe I have a natural talent for golf, but I also have a lot of other, more interesting things to do. So, I enjoyed 45 minutes of fun, graciously accepted the compliments of my teacher, and never set foot on the driving range again. Golf was for me a "garbage" activity; I had the potential but not the passion for it.

All activities that do not reach critical mass in relation to our desire to do them (even if we have the talent for them) qualify as **Garbage**. **What do you do with Garbage activities?** You throw them away. You let them go and never revisit them. We DVC's have a bunch of other interesting things we want to do.

"Time-bombs"

I bet you don't have any **"Time-bombs"** in your life. Getting paid to do something you despise *and* suck at, is a rare situation indeed.

What to do with "Time-bombs"? You get ready for the explosion, one that will adopt one of the following forms: you will get fired, or you will kicked out of business, any moment now.

However, there is a particular kind of "Time-bomb" out there, a very common one, inexorably ticking and ticking… they are called **Bad jobs**.

Bad Jobs

Everyone has or has had one. You have talent for it (or at least you have experience), and you get paid to do it… but you either are not too enthusiastic about it or you just plain hate it.

Bad jobs are a kind of "time-bomb" because the dissatisfaction they generate can be tolerated, but not forever. It builds up. If you deny the toll a bad job can take on your wellness at a medium term, it will eat you in the ways described back in Chapter 1 (depression, anger, and God knows what else).

What is it that makes it bad? It could be:
- Insufficient wage.
- Lack of advancement.

- Bad organizational climate (policies, culture, style).
- Bad organizational structure (e.g. too bureaucratic or autocratic).

Maybe is not the job that is bad, but only the company, or your boss, or the particular department your work for. Analyze if that "bad" job can be turned into a much better one by changing any of those variables.

The unequivocal sign of a Bad job is stress. Organizations generate stress in several ways:

- Bad relationship with the management.
- Bad supervision—unclear job demands, lack of autonomy/empowerment, insufficient or inadequate feedback.
- Role ambiguity—lack of stable job scope and responsibilities.
- Pressure to work too fast or too long: Excessive hours, inconvenient shifts… those are demands that sometimes do not even respond to real requirements of the job, but they are only a company culture thing; one that comes with a (veiled or explicit) threat: *"you either work more than you legally should, or get fired."*

And these are the physical and mental signs of being under job-related stress:[8]

- Low motivation to work
- Poor concentration on work tasks
- Poor work relationships with peers and supervisors
- Poor communications with others in the workplace
- Feelings of inadequacy or resentment
- Excessive tardiness or absenteeism

8: Magnusson (1990), Stress Management. Journal of Property Management.

What to do with a Bad job? You deactivate that "time-bomb" carefully, as if you were playing chess. You move your pieces quietly and intelligently until the time is right, and then you call checkmate.

What, concretely, are those moves?

First of all, you have to secure another job. If you are looking for a position in another company (you know the drill), you:

- Update your résumé. The help of a professional career consultant shouldn't be unaffordable and can make an *awesome* difference.

- Make a great presentation letter. They are used as a filtering system more than *résumés* themselves. I did it (literally) hundreds of times myself when selecting people for my team at IBM. The presentation letter shows how interested in a position a candidate really is—the résumé only says how qualified a candidate alleges to be. The more important the job, the more important the presentation letter becomes as a filtering resource.

- Look for opportunities in the job market, and send your papers *adapted to that particular position*: Not mass-mailing style, but surgically.

Again: the keywords here are "carefully deactivate". Don't go climbing and dancing naked on your boss's desk with the words "I QUIT" written on your buttocks, even if we know that you would enjoy doing that. Old bosses can get you ditched from a job selection process if someone happens to call them for references about you—unless you parted ways with that bad boss using a cordial farewell.

Private hobbies

So, you are long past 30 and love playing computer games or writing cheesy poetry? You can. Those are **Private Hobbies,** activities we are somewhat embarrassed to share, or for which we don't have talent, training, or experience, or activities that have no chance of yielding one dollar.

What to do with a Private Hobby? Enjoy it alone, of course, but watch out that it doesn't end up "eating" time, taking it away from the things that matter. Private hobbies are good to take your mind off things, but should only serve as a pause. Then you can get back to the "real deals" of your life.

Public hobbies

Public hobbies are among the great things of life. You enjoy them and you make new friends along the way. They usually take some money out of your pocket—and that's how it is supposed to be. A hobby is about having pleasure and unplugging from everyday problems and routine.

A hobby (public or private) does not necessarily have to be a typical one, like building model trains or collecting stamps. Those are perfectly okay, of course, but a DVC would, most likely, tend to choose hobbies that challenge and expand his talents; the same goes of course in regard to the professional activities we feel motivated to pursue.

What to do with a Public hobby?

Keep it and enjoy it. They are a realm of delight, a time to be like children again. And they are (sometimes) interesting candidates to become **missions** as well, in time.

Opportunities

Are you being paid to do something you like, but for which you have *no* talent (or at least not yet)?

DVC's don't usually have these, unless you are the lousy vice-president of a company owned by your dad, occupying an office as handsome as your assistants.

What do you do with your Opportunities? Maybe you have heard that the Chinese word for 'crisis' *(wēijī)* is formed by two Mandarin characters, one signifying "danger" and the other meaning "opportunity". Well, it seems that such thing is not true after all —that Chinese word just means *crisis*: "incipient moment; crucial point (when something begins or changes)".[9]

Think of **Opportunities** as a sort of *crisis*—an unstable situation. In short: get quickly better at it (acquire talent) or get ready to be replaced or muscled out of the market.

The mission of your life

We arrive, finally, at the center of the diagram. These are things you love, you have talent for, and you are (or could get) paid to do.

Have you found one of those? If not, don't worry. They are somewhere out there. But they are in disguise.

Look how **Bad jobs, Public hobbies**, and **Opportunities** are near the center of the diagram. They fulfill *two of the three* criteria required. Yes, even **Bad jobs**. Maybe having the same position in another company would improve things dramatically. Or maybe you have an "okay" job: reasonably well paid, reasonably satisfying, and you are reasonably good at it. Small adjustments can do the trick. Maybe.

A **Public hobby** could become your mission in life, but (and this is a big "but") you will have to learn how to monetize that activity. That is never easy.

An **Opportunity** is the most likely of the three to become the mission of your life: they are things you like and you get paid for. If you are lucky enough to be in such position, then all you have to do is to make a serious commitment to get really good at it.

Interpretation of results (big picture)

Take a long look at your spreadsheet: it is a representation of your real life and your potential life.

9: http://www.pinyin.info/chinese/crisis.html

Your personal results will have one of these forms:

- **You found one (and only one) Mission.** If you have only one activity identified as such, allow me congratulate you. That is, *according to your own present evaluation of inclinations, talents, and opportunities,* your mission in life.

- **You have too many Missions.** If you have four, five or more activities identified as **Missions** it may indicate that you were too generous with the scores you gave to your activities (not unusual at all: that's what we DVC's do). A new, more conservative scoring might be in order.

- **No activity qualified as a Mission.** If there is no activity at all in the center of the chart (that is, if you haven't rated any activity with a "3" or a "4" in all parameters), then one of the following has happened:

    1. You were too strict with the evaluation, most probably in regard to your talents or your abilities to monetize. Proposed solution: reconsider an adjustment in that category, reevaluating the activities again.

    2. You made an incomplete inventory of dreams. You haven't found activities with enough inclination AND enough business potential. Proposed solution: finish this book and keep thinking. Grow the inventory some more and try again.

    3. If you are sure you have made a complete list of dreams and that you were fair with the scoring, trust me: your mission is in there, very likely distributed among other activities, or disguised as something else. To uncover it, you will have to *synthesize it* from your top-rated activities.

Think of **Missions** (and **opportunities**, too) as diamonds in the rough: they need to be "polished"—questioned, analyzed, and defined with more precision.

Either that, or you have a hidden mission that needs uncovering. In both cases, the next step is the same. And that step (in the very next paragraphs) embodies the core of this book: **the cure for the DVC.**

So for the moment, your Excel sheet looks like this:

A	B	C	D	E	F	G
	INVENTORY OF DREAMS	Wish	Talent	Money		RESULTS
1	Learning to play harpsichord	2	3	1		Garbage
2	Playing tennis	2	2	4		Time Bomb
3	Obtaining my license as masseur	2	3	2		Garbage
4	Start my own business (used books store)	4	4	2		Public Hobby
5	Start my own business (vintage bike parts)	3	1	2		Private hobby
6	Learning to draw portraits	4	4	4		Mission
7	Finish my novel and submit it to a writing contest	3	2	2		Private hobby
8	Current job: customer sat supervisor at Initech	4	4	4		Mission
9	Current side job: building handmade pipes	3	3	3		Mission
10	Current hobby 1: Bycicle riding twice a week	3	2	1		Private hobby

A complex, multi-sided specialization

Curses are not diseases; they don't go away with medicines, they don't go away with spells. They go away with action.

We DVC's must not settle on finding a specialization: we must discover one that combines our stronger interests, our best talents and our best chances of profitability. And the **Missions** you just identified are the leading candidates.

What is more: since we are forced to play the specialization game, we might as well play it in our own style, which is "specific but heterogeneous". It consists of the following steps:

1. "Synthesizing" a stimulating specialization, which...

2. ...takes elements from more than one traditional field, and...

3. ... is complemented by other activities to create a balanced, challenging, and stimulating portfolio of activities.

Example from my own life. I have chosen to be a *luthier*—a maker of stringed musical instruments. Remember how specific my last book was (the one on electric guitar design)? Well, this profession is *specific*, but also *heterogeneous*: I apply knowledge related to engineering, electronics, acoustics, design, ergonomics, woodworking, and so on. *Lutherie* demands from me precise handwork ability, a finely tuned aesthetic sense, and the stamina needed to be my own sales manager as well. And then I write books on the subject.

What is the combination of "specific and heterogeneous" that works for you?

Maybe such activity is not written on *one* particular line of our inventory of dreams: at this point it might be scattered among two or three of those activities, waiting for a connection to be made inside your head.

We are far from done. Before building your portfolio of activities (chapter 11), and further defining (polishing, synthesizing) your mission, you have to know:

- What **work style** is the best for you
- What **area of knowledge** is the best for you
- What **role** is the best for you.
- What **work environment** is the best for you

And now you tell me? How am I supposed to know all that?

Patience, Neville. We have to break our own *Petrificus Totalus* step by step.

10
Work Styles, Areas, Roles

[SABRINA FAIRCHILD (Audrey Hepburn) has fled to Paris to study *haute cuisine*, in an attempt to forget her infatuation with David Larrabee. The teacher, a French CHEF (Marcel Hillaire) with a huge nose, a huge hat, and a pointy moustache, starts the lesson of the day, speaking with a strong French accent.]

CHEF: *Bonjour, mes dames et messieurs. Yesterday we have learnt the correct way how to boil water. Today we will learn the correct way how to crack an egg.*

[HE PRODUCES AN EGG] *Voilà, an egg!*

Now, an egg is not a stone; it is not made of wood. It is a living thing, with a heart. So when we crack it, we must not torment it. We must be merciful and execute it quickly, like with the guillotine —Tzack! You see? It is all in the wrist. One, two, three: Crack!

[HE WALKS DOWN THE ROOM SUPERVISING THE STUDENTS, WHO CRACK EGGS. HE REACHES SABRINA'S TABLE —SHE IS NOT CRACKING ANY EGGS. HE STARES AT HER INQUISITIVELY, AND SHE SHOWS HIM A DESTROYED EGG ON HER HAND. HE INSTRUCTS:]

The wrist! Like a whip! You watch: New egg!

[HE TAKES AN EGG TO SHOW HER] One, two, three: Crack!

[THE EGG COMPLETELY DESTROYS IN HIS HAND, TOO. EMBARRASSED, HE HIDES IT BEHIND HIS BACK AND ORDERS]

CHEF: New egg!

(From "Sabrina" — Directed by Billy Wilder, 1954.)

Quick recap: By now, you have a list of activities rated according to your own inclinations, talents, and financial potential:

- **Bad jobs, "Time Bombs"** and **Garbage,** which need to be disposed of.

- **Private hobbies** and **Public hobbies**, which beg to be enjoyed. Select one, if you must. It's okay.
- **Missions,** which need to be worked on—i.e. they have to be polished (defined more precisely) or synthesized (unified with other activities disguised as **Opportunities**).

Next steps

To polish/synthesize those activities, we will go through three steps of identifying your preferred **work style**, preferred **area of knowledge**, and preferred **role**. At the end, you should have a clearer idea of what your mission should look like.

1. Our preferred work style

Surely you have heard of research conducted in recent years that identified different kind of intelligences. For example, there are people who are recognized as brilliant because they excel at logic and mathematics. Ask them to address an auditorium full of people, though, and—provided they can summon enough courage—they will bore that audience into deep drowsiness. Conversely, a natural-born entertainer can have the audience laughing and enjoying in no time. But ask *him* to demonstrate the simplest of theorems and enjoy watching him running to the hills.

By definition, a DVC has more than one type of intelligence. We don't fit 100% in any particular intelligence type; we fit, to a relatively high degree, in several types. For example, we DVC's may not necessarily have perfect pitch, but we have musical instinct ; we are not math geniuses, but our mental processes are structured around a logical perception of the world; we might not be born-entertainers, but we know our ways regarding interaction with other people.

And that is precisely the core of the Da Vinci Curse. Imagine a person with a strong kinetic intelligence (she's good with his body) and just an *average* level of other intelligences. Such person will be naturally inclined to (she will crave, she will enjoy, and she will be good at) activities with a physical component: sports, dance, performing arts, jobs that require strength, resistance, precision, and good timing. She could make an excellent athlete, combat pilot, actor, choreographer, builder, police officer, soldier, even a surgeon. But many a DVC could be as good as the "pure-kinetic" type if she just had the constancy and focus to pursue a kinetic activity. And that is the core of our problem: becoming an athlete or a dancer would conspire against cultivating activities that could be *simultaneously* related to the two, three, or four types of intelligence we have. Identifying our preferred "work style" means identifying which intelligence types we have and prefer to use.

Can you find your style in the following table? (Intelligence cannot be summarized in a table; take this just as a practical generalization) [10]:

Type of intelligence	Talent areas and activities
Logical-mathematical *("good with numbers")*	Formal logic, abstract concepts, reasoning, math, computer programming, reasoning, pattern recognition, scientific thinking, complex calculations. **They learn best by:** Analyzing.
Spatial *("good with objects")*	Visualizing thought, spatial judgment, artistic sense, shapes, geometry, and relation between objects. Interconnectivity, mechanic, and dynamic aspects of matter in a spatial context. **They learn best by:** Visualizing and imagining.
Linguistic *("good with words")*	Facility with words and languages. Writing, explaining, teaching, discussing, verbally expressing. Ability to understand and manipulate syntax and structure. **They learn best by:** Reading and listening.

10: I have created this table based on several others of the kind —not my own research, though.

Kinetic *("good with the body")*	Control of one's bodily motions and the capacity to handle diverse objects skillfully. Sense of physical timing, of physical action, ability to train responses so they become reflexes. **They learn best by:** Doing, touching, acting out.
Auditory *("good with sounds")*	Sensitivity to sounds, rhythms, tones, pitch, meter, melody and timbre. Ability to sing, to play musical instruments, and to compose. **They learn best by:** Listening.
Interpersonal *("good with people")*	Communication abilities, empathy. Ability to understand others: their moods, feelings, temperaments, and motivations.1 **They learn best by:** Working with others.
Intrapersonal *("good with ideas")*	Introspective and self-reflective capacities. Philosophical and critical thinking. People with this intelligence are, most likely: authors, psychologists, counselors, philosophers, and members of the clergy. **They learn by:** Reflecting on things.
Naturalistic *("good with nature")*	Inclination to understand and interact with natural elements and/or live things. Geology, biology, farming, biochemistry are typical examples of the career choices of people with this intelligence. **They learn best by:** Observing and classifying.

Did you find your preferred work styles? I bet you did: almost all of them, right? That's so da Vinci cursed! But remember, we are looking for a couple of them, your top two or three. Keep them in mind for what follows.

2. Our preferred <u>area of knowledge</u>

We define a "dream job" as a job aligned with our **Mission**. Having such a job is a rare privilege. Getting to it might take time and effort (training, obtaining experience, and finally getting a job offer for it), but it is not impossible. Finding yourself sooner or later in position to aim for a job like that in a reasonable timeframe should be *logical*. Not easy, but logical.

The graphic on the next page is a taxonomy of jobs, grouped in six basic areas: Action-oriented, people-oriented, organization-oriented, and so on. Each area makes use of specific types of intelligence, i.e. work styles. Note also that the *intersections* between basic areas define sub-areas—jobs that demand talents on more than one single area (that sounds like us, doesn't it?) In what areas/sub-areas would you say that a dream job for you would be located (even if it is not written in there)? Take a look.

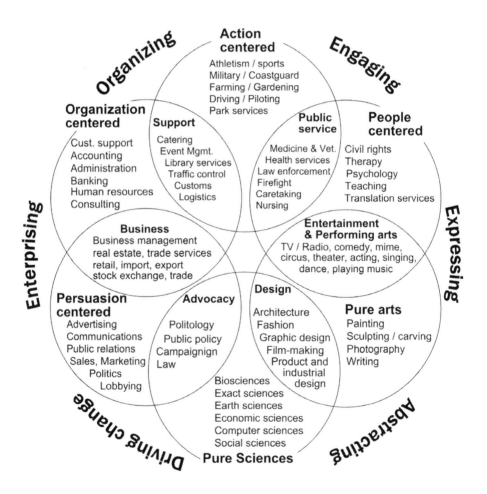

The chart is not an Ouija board; no magic answers lie in there. It is more like a compass. It may not point to a "perfect job", but it shows the available directions. Also, be aware that the chart is merely indicative, not exhaustive:

- **Each category represents many other jobs.** The category "Business", for example, shows only a few areas (management, real estate, retail, etc.), but business endeavors adopt a myriad of modalities.

- **Each area represents many related oc-cupations.** "Medicine & Vet", for example, encompasses a huge variety of specialties (radiology, surgery, and dozens more—remember the "Swiss Cheese expert"?)

I haven't explored jobs that could involve *three* categories simultaneously. They *do* exist, and they are probably close to what we defined as the cure for the Da Vinci curse. In that spirit, however, feel free to try to figure out possible jobs encompassing three areas you are especially talented for, trained in, and interested in working on.

Note that opposing circles also represent opposing orientations. They are not necessarily incompatible; they just require *opposite* work styles (and/or intelligence types).

An organization-based job ("northwest" in the chart) requires order, planning, method, timed-action; while a work in pure arts ("southeast"), despite involving specific techniques, may well benefit from chaotic, inspired, spontaneous-action.

In the same way, people-centered jobs ("northeast") have people as an *end*, while persuasion-oriented jobs ("southwest") have people as a *medium*—to sell them something, to get someone elected, or to encourage charitable programs that save people, too.

Finally, pure-science jobs ("south") deal with abstract entities (numbers, formulas, principles) while action-oriented jobs ("north") deal with real and present situations, sometimes dangerous, always physical.

Locate these two variables in the chart:

1. The general direction of your **interests**
2. The general direction of your present **skills**

One of the following things will happen:

If your interests and your skills are aligned, then you might have a bad-job problem.

If your interests and skills are more or less in the vicinity of each other, you can define your re-training needs and make a plan to transition into the desired area.

If your interests and skills point in opposite directions (for example you have training as a scientist, but you long to be a musician), then one of the following options open up:

- Unless you are relatively young, your interest might have to be carried out as a hobby.
- If that interest *must* become your life-long-project... well, that's a problem that needs careful consideration.

I hope you don't fall within this last case, but da Vinci cursed people usually does. Maybe you just evaluated your interest in a non-realistic way, making yourself believe that you want to jump headfirst into some new cool thing that just crossed your mind (typical DVC, right?) Let the enthusiasm decant. Research the desired activity, investigate how it would be like to exercise it professionally, and then reconsider the whole thing again.

But if the suspicion happens to be true after all (i.e. you have conducted your life in such a self-sabotaging way as to let yourself be carried towards the opposite direction of your interests and desires), then you face a path that will have to be managed taking care of yourself and the people that depend on you; drastic changes can be disruptive; they need planning, patience, and dedication.

More likely, your experience and your interests will not be perfectly aligned, either: chances are they more or less overlap, so some negotiation between them will have to take place.

There are two ways to increase the alignment between your interests and your experience:

- **Acquiring new skills** and gradually gaining new experience. You will have to read books, read web contents, take part in courses, receive individual training, talk to experts in the area, review journals, specialized literature, etc., etc.

- **Adapting / redefining your interests** so they can be approached making the best possible use of your current experience.

For instance, imagine that a policeman wants to work in event-management—two areas not opposite, but not perfectly aligned either. A logical entry point to the new activity would be (at least initially) to focus in the security-related aspects of event organization. Or, for example, if you have worked as a salesperson all your life but are drawn to art, opening an art gallery (dealing with artworks, interacting with artists) is a "safer" start: you do something you are familiar with, while improving your artistic skills enough until you place your own paintings for sale, too. It certainly would be wiser than to throw everything away and start painting for your living.

3. Our preferred <u>roles</u>

Back in chapter 1 we reviewed the "vertical world" basic roles: philosophers, scientists, designers, engineers, marketers, artists, critics... etc.

Those tags are generalizations, but in any case: in which of those **roles** you think you would feel more comfortable? Your answer should be in line with your preferred "work style" and "area of knowledge".

The word "role" is a close synonym with "specialization". The role you better fit is a defining characteristic of your dream job. For that, consider these questions:

What role can you better *sell*? A good way to find our ideal role is to imagine that we are *salespersons*. Everyone is selling. Philosophers sell ideas, scientists sell research projects, designers sell prototypes, engineers sell know-how, and marketers sell anything. In which role could you more easily pitch your work to investors, customers, sponsors, etc.?

What role is definitely not a fit for you? Define which roles you will avoid. The key concept here is outsourcing: hiring others to do what you suck at, or that which makes you feel miserable. Take advantage of other people's specialization by delegating what they can do better than you. It will also give you more time to focus on your core business.

And finally, define in which fronts you will compete. Just as no company can capture all customers in all markets, your "heterogeneous specialization" must focus on the aspects in which your talents can actually give you a competitive advantage.

Example: the wine Yellow Tail. It went from nothing to top-selling wine in the US in just two years. It beat both the high-quality wines and the cheapest ones by avoiding confrontation in the classical fronts: volume of advertising, quality of maturation, complexity, and variety of offers. Yellow Tail differentiated itself by offering an excellent price vs. quality, an easy-to-drink wine, and an easy-to-choose bottle (with funny colors and a Kangaroo in the label). Compared with the rest of the market (the people already doing what you want to do), what is going to be *your* "Kangaroo" (your differentiating proposition)?

4. Your preferred work environment

Do you prefer working...

- **Indoors or outdoors?** (A no-brainer for people with a "naturalistic" intelligence type)

- **In a physically active job, or a more sedentary one?**
- **Mostly alone, or mostly with other people?** (Are you an introverted or an extroverted person?)
- **In a quiet environment, or with high interactivity?** (A matter of personal rhythm).
- **Having autonomy of decisions, or under clear guidance?** (Each one implies particular responsibilities).
- **In a predictable, routine fashion, or under conditions that require improvisation?**

Now consider **how important is for you...**

- **Working in a company with high ethical standards?** (Environmental, personal, social, moral, etc.)
- **Having other people under your supervision?** (Transcend the "thrill" of being the boss: with oversight of personnel a lot of menial tasks come along, too, and you become instantly responsible for everything that happens in your team, even the small stuff).
- **Having chances of career advancement?** (Consider the things that come with that besides the bigger paycheck: personnel under your responsibility and more hours. The company's smartphone, car, and notebook are nice, but they are also ways to make you work faster, harder, and longer).

Back to square one

Allow me to introduce a last tweak in this chapter about "polishing" your dream job.

We define an ***objective*** as: 1) An intention, 2) to be accomplished to a certain degree or measure, 3) within a specified timeframe, 4) with a certain priority.

If I say that I plan to do the following:

"Going to the gym."

"Eating more vegetables."

"Jogging."

...then I have no objectives at all. Those are not even tasks; they are just good intentions.

But if I say:

"I will go to the gym for an hour, twice a week, for 6 months."

"I will reduce the intake of fats, meat, and sugar as much as possible, for 60 days and see the impact on the scale."

"I will walk/jog for 30 minutes, three times a week, until the beginning of winter."

...well, that sounds much better.

So, your homework now is to take your Missions (and also your **Opportunities** and **Hobbies,** if you want) **and understand them as** *objectives*: **what do you want to accomplish, to what degree, in how much time.**

No big deal. John Lennon said *"life is what happens to you while you are making other plans"*. Leading a complete and successful life is an *ideal*, something we can only *approach*. Our lives are *real*—far from perfect.

"Planning" is the base of it, but to achieve a decent balance among several activities requires discipline and perseverance. And the next chapter is about precisely that.

You know, it's all in the wrist.

11

Life Balance: Maslow's Pyramid, With a Twist

> [First interview between ALBERT MARKOWSKI (Jason Schwartzman) and VIVIAN JAFFE (Lily Tomlin). She is an "existential detective", who ALBERT wants to hire in order to find out about a series of strange coincidences that have happened to him lately.]
>
> [VIVIAN] *Why don't you just tell me what your situation is?*
>
> [ALBERT] *Look, I'm not sure what you guys do, all right?*
>
> [VIVIAN] *Well, we will investigate and solve your case.*
>
> [ALBERT] *How?*
>
> [VIVIAN] *If you sign a contract, we'll follow you.*
>
> [ALBERT] *You'll spy on me?*
>
> [VIVIAN] *Yes.*
>
> [ALBERT] *Will you be spying on me in the bathroom?*
>
> [VIVIAN] *Yes.*
>
> [ALBERT] *In the bathroom?!*
>
> [VIVIAN] *Yes.*
>
> [ALBERT] *Why?*
>
> [VIVIAN] *There's nothing too small. Do you know when the police find the slightest bit of DNA and build a case on it? If we might see you floss or masturbate, that could be the key to your entire reality.*
>
> **(From "I Heart Huckabee's", Directed by David O. Russell, 2004.)**

This chapter is a short one, but an important read before we get to build your new portfolio of activities.

I am sure you heard about "Maslow's pyramid", a graphical interpretation of **Abraham Maslow**'s theory of the hierarchy of human needs.

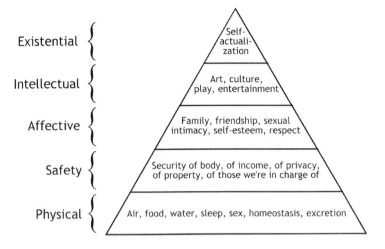

An interesting revalation: *our behavior in life centers on the lowest of the unsatisfied levels.* The levels above that unsatisfied one are neglected or even denied. But as soon as the need we had is fairly well satisfied a need placed on the level immediately above emerges, capturing our focus. For example, if we are starving, there is little we can do until that vital need is satisfied, and so on.

Maslow didn't actually draw a *pyramid*; he just described a *hierarchy* of needs in a scientific paper, so all those pyramids are interpretations of his words.

Some pyramids introduce a level for "self-esteem"; I bet that happened back in the 1980s, when that concept started to spawn self-help bestsellers. Someone else elbowed in "transcendence" at the very top (a word not present at all in the original paper). So, when you google the words "Maslow pyramid", you get a million different versions in 0.7 seconds. Maslow did put "Self-actualization" at the top, though—*that* being precisely his main point.

The lower layers are wider and closer to the base; that means that those areas are more *fundamental* in a biological/psychological sense; it doesn't necessarily mean that they require more conscious focus. The very base of the pyramid (level 1), the "physiological needs", is the biggest of them all, but we satisfy all those things more or less automatically, while we concentrate a lot more as we go up the pyramid.

Focus/balance: an unsolvable trade-off?

"Focus" means to put our energy and attention in one particular thing. "Balance" means to distribute that energy and attention among several things. And both are sold as "virtues". *Should we concentrate on one thing, or on several? How to solve this trade-off?*

There is an *inverse* relation between the quantity of activities we engage, and the amount of focus we can assign to each of them.

These relations are shown in figure 11 below from another standpoint (they are described here using the normal, positive term and also a "Shadow" term. One behavior can be good or not, depending on its reasons and effects:

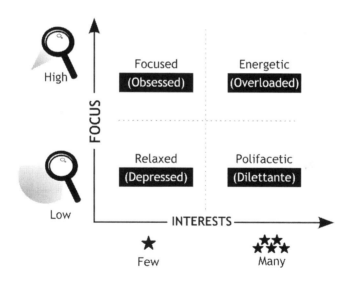

Figure 11: Number of interests versus the energy available for each of them.

Balance is achieved somewhere in the middle of the chart, where a fair number of interests or areas receive a fair amount of the energy and focus we have available. Such delicate equilibrium is not easy to achieve or to sustain, but it is possible to make adjustments in order to approximate a more balanced life.

Stereotypical, unbalanced pyramids

Let's simplify the pyramid levels to only three: **body, mind,** and **spirit,** in that ascending order. If your life lacks exercise, sex, health, or adequate nutrition, you have a deficit in the *body* level. The *mind* level refers to work, intellect, and entertainment. And the *spirit* level refers to emotion, love, self-actualization (individuation), etc.

So considered, the following are some stereotypical pyramids. Do you recognize yourself in any of these?

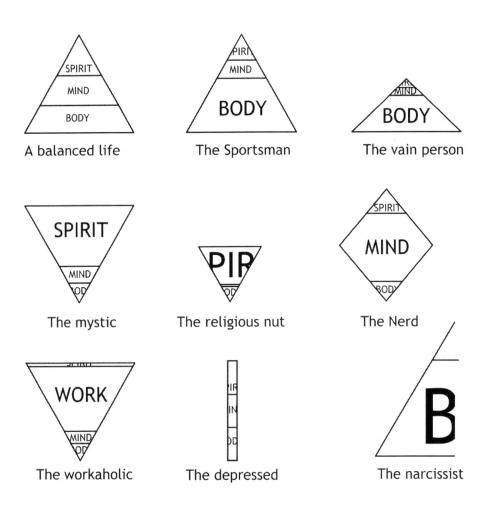

Note how an incorrect balance of energy investment in the three areas generates "unstable" pyramids (an elegant way to say "incomplete life" or even worse: "premature death").

What does your pyramid lack?

In other words: What would make your portfolio more balanced? What's missing in your daily routine, whether you miss it or not? Exercise, reading, meditation, a vegan diet, a little sex?

Each life is a different universe; so please do the following, applied to your own personal situation:

Identify your current <u>deficits</u>, include them in your activity list (the dream inventory in Excel) and score all three columns with a "3", by decree.

Remember, these are not specific events (like "read book X"), but ongoing activities (like "increase my knowledge of subject 'A' by reading books X, Y, and Z").

A balanced life is formed by big things, small ones, things we need, things we want, things we would prefer not to do. None of those things by itself constitutes the key to your entire reality, but the complete set of them certainly does.

12

Your Portfolio Of Activities: Cows, Dogs, and Rising Stars

> [CHUCKIE (Ben Affleck) finally confronts his best friend WILL HUNTING (Matt Damon) at the construction yard. WILL is a boy genius who is wasting his extraordinary abilities because he does not feel a duty to himself to utilize them.]
>
> [CHUCKIE] Look, you're my best friend, so don't take this the wrong way. But in twenty years, if you're livin' next door to me, comin' over, watchin' the fuckin' Patriots' games and still workin' construction, I'll fuckin' kill you. And that's not a threat, that's a fact. I'll fuckin' kill you.
>
> [WILL] Chuckie, what are you talkin'--
>
> [CHUCKIE] Fuck you. You owe it to me. Tomorrow I'm gonna wake up and I'll be fifty and I'll still be doin' this. And that's all right 'cause I'm gonna make a run at it. But you... you're sittin' on a winning lottery ticket and you're too much of a pussy to cash it in. And that's bullshit 'cause I'd do anything to have what you got. And so would any of these guys. It'd be a fuckin' insult to us all if you're still here in twenty years.
>
> (From "Good Will Hunting", Directed by Gus Van Sant, 1997.)

Time for another quick recap. You have identified potential **missions, hobbies,** and **opportunities.** You have identified complementary activities that build up a nice personal pyramid.

Now, it is time to put these in concert with each other, that is, we must take that group of activities and organize them into a "portfolio". Our portfolio is based on a classic management tool, the "BCG Matrix", developed by the Boston Consulting Group to help business conglomerates decide which companies to keep and which to get rid of. It compares two parameters: the market growth rate, and the market share of a particular company. Evaluated in such a way, they get classified as:

Stars: companies in the group with a *high* market share in an *expanding* market. Their performance is bound to be excellent. These have to be kept at all costs.

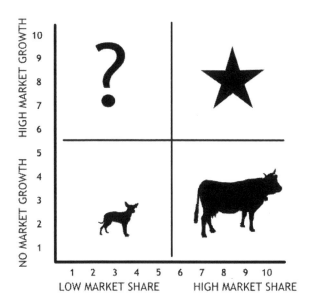

Cash cows: companies with high market share, but in a *contracting* market. These have to be kept as long as they continue producing money. They help finance the rest of the companies.

Pets: companies with *low* presence in a *contracting* market. Sometimes called "dead dogs", they have to be gotten rid of quickly because they stink, or will soon (a metaphor for "losing money").

Dilemmas: companies with low market share, but in an *expanding* market. The "dilemma" is to decide whether to invest in them or not.

All markets have a cycle (*start, expand, stabilize*, and sooner or later *decline*), and companies follow a cycle as well: "Stars" turn (in time) into "cash cows", and cash cows turn into "dead dogs" (**Bad-jobs** do too).

The last step

Now it is time to make the last evaluation in this book. **Rate your top activities ("Missions" and "Opportunities") from 1 to 10, in the two last columns:**

- **The actual and current contribution to your personal finances.** Is this activity an *asset* (does it put money in your pocket) or a *liability* (it takes money out of your pocket)? If it takes a lot of money from you, give it a "1". If it gives you *all* of your money, give it a "10" (try not to rate them with a "5", so they end up clearly classified in some quadrant).

- **Contribution to your personal actualization**—how crucial you feel this particular activity is regarding your individuation, self-actualization, happiness, etc.?

<u>Important:</u> Rate your current job in those two columns, too. Yes, especially if it is a **Bad job.**

After the evaluation, your Excel sheet looks like this:

A	B	C	D	E	F	G	H	I
							Actual and current contribution to finances	Contribution to your personal individuation
	INVENTORY OF DREAMS	Wish	Talent	Money		RESULTS		
1	Learning to play harpsichord	2	4	1		Garbage		
2	Playing tennis	3	2	1		Private hobby		
3	Obtain my license as masseur	4	4	3		Mission	6	8
4	Used book store	3	2	3		Opportunity	1	7
5	Vintage bike parts	3	2	2		Private hobby		
6	Learning to draw portraits	3	2	1		Private hobby		
7	Finish novel	2	3	1		Garbage		
8	Current work at Initech	1	3	4		Bad job	7	2
9	Handmade pipes	3	4	2		Public Hobby	3	6
10	Bycicle riding	3	3	3		Mission	1	1

Note that we are not considering **"Time Bombs"** and **Garbage** anymore: I hope you got rid of those long ago. **Private Hobbies** are not relevant for this analysis, either; you can score your principal **Public Hobby** though—you never know if a chance to monetize them will show up in the future.

Once all activities have been rated, go to the *Sheet 2* of your Excel (click the "Sheet2" tab in the lower left of your screen (marked with an arrow):

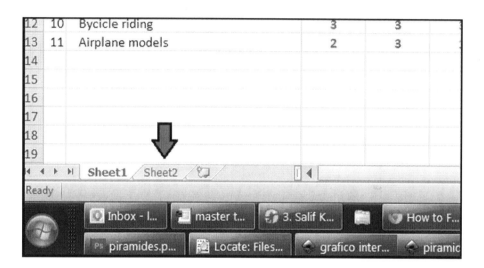

In that second sheet, you will find a graphic that should look like figure 16 (on next page). There you will have all **Missions, Opportunities, Hobbies, Bad Jobs**, and other complementary activities (those that balance your pyramid) placed on the different quadrants.

The most important are, of course, the **stars.** If you have more than one of those, do not engage simultaneously, because they can beat the crap out of your agenda and your life balance. If you have more than one "star", you will have to do one of the following:

- Choose one and keep the rest in a drawer—or downgrade them to "hobbies".

- Exercise your decision-making skills, and knock them down one by one, each at their own time.

- Synthesize a new mission with elements from all of them, if at all possible.

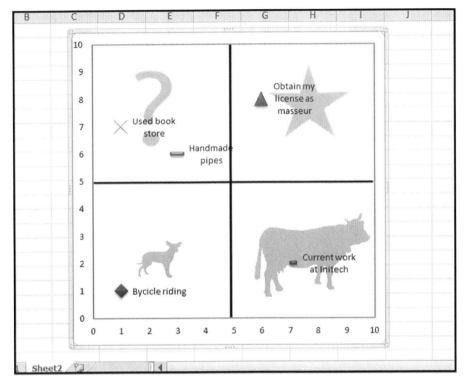

Figure 16: Your portfolio of activities (it would be moreo populated than this one—this is just an example).

(In my personal chart I had three activities in the **Stars** quadrant. One of them was writing this book; now I am going after the other two.)

Now, this is what you do with the rest of them:

Dilemmas: research and decide whether you want to pursue them or not, and to what extent. The "dilemmas' quadrant" will be most likely populated by **"Opportunities"**. Remember: each hour you dedicate to these "pies in the sky" is an hour that your "Stars" lose.

Cash Cows: Your "bad job" is somewhere in the cash cow quadrant, for sure. It may not contribute much to your happiness, but it pays the bills. You proceed with it as discussed: keep doing it until it is safe to let it go, or until it turns into a "dead dog"—something so damaging to your well-being that taking action cannot be postponed any longer.

Pets: Activities you don't like to do but which you need to do should have ended up in this part of the graphic. These are "pets", not "dead dogs". Hopefully you will have none of these. You can have one "pet", of course (a hobby that you love to do without any hope of making a career out of it); just like a real pets, hobbies provide joy to your life. But two, three, or more of them become increasingly demanding. Ideally, your new discovered "Star" will become your hobby, so you can really put all your focus in it. Remember: hobbies are trying to perpetuate the curse. If you end up with two or more of such lesser activities in your portfolio, don't let them distract you: put them quickly out of their misery.

13

Pendings: Just Business

> SABRINA FAIRCHILD (Julia Ormond) and millionaire LINUS LARRABEE (Harrison Ford) are headed to Martha's Vineyard, as part of a stratagem of LINUS aimed at keeping SABRINA away from his brother David. They walk from the helicopter into the private plane.]
>
> [LINUS] [POINTING BACK AT THE HELICOPTER] *It saves us all that time fighting traffic.*
>
> [SABRINA] *Don't you ever look out the window?*
>
> [LINUS] *When I have time.*
>
> [SABRINA] *What happened to the time you saved by taking the helicopter?*
>
> [LINUS] [SMILING CLEVERLY] *I'm storing it up.*
>
> [SABRINA] [SADDENED BUT FIRMLY] *No, you're not.*
>
> [LINUS] [TRYING TO MAKE CONVERSATION] *So... "Sabrina" is a beautiful name. How did you get it?*
>
> [SABRINA] *From my father's readings. It's in a poem. It's this story of a water sprite who saved a virgin from a fate of waste and death.*
>
> [LINUS] *And Sabrina is the virgin.*
>
> [SABRINA] [LOOKING OUT THE WINDOW] *Sabrina is the savior.*
>
> **(From "Sabrina", directed by Sidney Pollack, 1995.)**

"*Just Business*", read an insurance company poster I saw once. It had the photo of a majestic bald eagle's head looking at you, serious and self-confident. That's how I believe pendings have to be confronted.

There are many, many time-management systems out there. Among the commercially oriented ones, promises of *"taking definitive control of your 'to-do' lists"* and even *"taking control of your life"* are not uncommon. It is a business, after all, one that generates millions in sales of books, seminars, agendas, etc.

But *all* time-management systems (TMS's from now on) have some inherent limitations:

- **TMS's do not manage time.** They are "garbage in/garbage out" systems. They only can help you organize your to-do's if you first set priorities correctly, record them appropriately, etc. Bad prioritization results in lousy time management.
- **TMS's cannot manage you, either.** They do not provide discipline: they *require* discipline. The system itself demands time and effort, which are precisely the things they are supposed to *save*.

Understanding pendings

Time is the scarce resource par excellence. Money comes and goes, love comes and goes, and luck comes and goes. But time just goes away. *Pendings* are things that demand our attention; rarely will we have enough time to do them all. And some of them we shouldn't do, at all. Consequently, we need some criteria to value each pending on our to-do list. I propose here the most objective, no-nonsense way I found.

Urgency and importance

The essential attribute of pendings is their **priority.** Priority is defined by the combination of different degrees of **urgency** and **importance**.

If we say that something is "urgent", we are saying that it requires attention soon; we are not saying anything about that attention being deserved at all. Modern life is full of unimportant urgencies.

From an "importance" standpoint, pendings can oscillate between *essential* and *trivial*.

Let's see how the combination of these parameters defines the priority of a pending. The following are extreme cases; all other possibilities lie in the middle.

Extremely urgent and important: Emergencies

The word "emergency" and the verb "to emerge" have the same root: We are going on with our lives as usual, and then something that requires our immediate and undivided attention shows up. Emergencies do not always have to be negative, but they usually are—or will become so if we don't act.

Being terribly late for a meeting or a movie is *not* an emergency. Emergencies are situations *that present a clear and present danger to us or to other people*. Anything that can be explained and apologized for over the phone is not an emergency.

What to do during emergencies: Emergencies need three things from us, in this precise order: **calm, focus,** and **action.** Emergencies require the suspension of all other non-critical pendings. The only active and conscious stance required from us is to do our best to stay calm; to counterbalance adrenaline with a cool head.

There are a huge variety of emergencies, but a rational sequence of action, whatever the nature of the emergency, would be:

1. **Give the alarm**. Ask for help, scream, press the fire alarm button, dial 911, or whatever is available.
2. **If necessary, protect yourself from the cause of the danger** so you can help others at the scene, or going for help.
3. **Fight or flight**, depending on the situation.

The word "emergency" sounds catastrophic, but even small things can escalate into that category: an egg left unattended on the stove will cook, and then burn, and then it may cause a fire.

Urgent, non-important: everyday stuff

These are "time-critical" things, but the world will not end if we don't do them on time: in general, they just imply a higher cost in the future (in terms of money, time, reputation, etc.).

The supermarket closes in 10 minutes, and all I have in the refrigerator is half a lemon. If I don't focus on getting there soon I will end up ordering a pizza, which is more expensive, less healthy, and less tasty than what I can fix myself in a few minutes (I enjoy cooking, a lot). If you don't pay the cell-phone bill on time, they will cancel the service. No catastrophe will ensue, but setbacks will: penalties, having to use pay phones, and maybe losing opportunities because of unreturned calls.

Time-critical pendings are pendings of different urgency that have a precise point in the future: meetings, dates, programmed events, etc. Their time criticality is normally a consequence of agreements with other people. Their importance resides both in the events themselves, and in how they affect your reputation as a dependable person.

What to do with time-critical pendings? First, create a good agenda and organize appointments realistically. Then, be on time —better 5 minutes early than 5 minutes late. If you have to cancel or reschedule, do it as soon as you realize the need for a change. Pick up the phone, apologize, and renegotiate.

Non-urgent but important

I remember a comic strip by Quino, a beloved humorist from Argentina. His character, Mafalda—a six-year-old girl— observes a group of working men digging a hole on the pavement on her way to school. She stops, then gets closer and asks them: *"Are you looking for the roots of our national identity?"* One of the men answers: *"What? No, kid, we are looking for a gas leak"*. Mafalda reflects, resigned: *"It's always the same... Urgent things don't leave any time for the important ones!"*

Important things can get overtaken by day-to-day, "urgent" things that need to be done, but which do not contribute to our individuation.

"Non-urgent" does not mean "unimportant". Classic example: time spent with loved ones—"non-urgent" moments that will never come back.

Non-urgent/non-important: Trivia

I relate trivia to entertainment. If I don't go to the movies today, I can always go later, or buy the DVD and watch it home in a couple of months.

Talking about trivia, in the next chapter I will go deeper regarding things that receive much more attention from us than they deserve.

Precedence

Some things have to be taken care of before others; not because they are more important, but because they are *requisites*: there are timing reasons, cost reasons, convenience reasons.

Gantt diagrams are a tool classically used in project management. They order different tasks and events on a timeline, organized by their mutual precedence; once completed, a Gantt diagram shows the optimal way of accomplishing those tasks. Some of them can be done simultaneously; others cannot begin until some previous one is completed. The curious thing about time-management systems is that few of them include a Gantt-like feature, so precedence and priorities are unclear.

Big, ugly, hairy things

There is a type of pending that doesn't fit in any of the categories above: the big, ugly, hairy things that stay on our "to-do" list forever.

I think I have found the reason: they are not *one* pending, they are actually *several*, and we lack information about them. Information is the base of decision making, and "big, hairy pendings" cannot be dealt with unless their components and precedents are understood.

Examples of "big, hairy pendings" are:

- Things we are not sure when (or even whether) must be done.
- Things we deny somehow (in my personal case: medical procedures of any kind).

- Things loosely defined; things only expressed as intentions, not yet as objectives.

What to do with big, hairy pendings? Well, if lack of information is the problem, then the solution is *communication*—that's how information is acquired. You have to talk to someone.

- **An advisor**—your lawyer, your doctor, your tax person.
- **An insider**—a customer-support representative, a public officer, an information desk, a friend who went through that.
- **A stakeholder**—those expecting you to complete that task. It can be your boss, your spouse, your children, a neighbor, a government office, a company, etc.

They should help you understand if that particular task is important, urgent, both, or neither. Of course, in order to get an objective assessment, make sure that the person you are consulting is on *your* side. Don't ask a casino owner about the best way of investing your life's savings.

Attitude regarding pendings

Here I list some useful advice regarding pendings. Use those you find applicable to your personal situation.

- **Do not work with an artificial sense of urgency**. A pretty standard attitude these days, one I have perceived first hand, especially in American corporations. The competition among peers for raises and promotions fuels a default, artificial sense of urgency that seeks to "demonstrate" one's identification with the company. Paradoxically, employees who are conscious of their own limitations (serenely and rationally pushing back requests that they are not in a position to satisfy, or asking for additional resources) show the character and realistic attitude that upper management considers indicative of potential executives.

- **Forget the "wow!" factor.** Do not try to amaze other people anymore. In particular, bosses don't like to be surprised—not even positively. They want to be kept informed of your progress, instead. Not knowing what is going on puts them in a vulnerable position in front of *their* bosses. Let important stakeholders in your life know (partners included) what you are up to—except maybe for surprise anniversary gifts.

- **Minimize "changing horses in midstream".** Decide a way to go, and stick to it—unless the path proves to be unviable or extremely costly. Real time optimization is for car sat-navs. For people, it means losing focus on the goal. Instead of changing strategies constantly, learn for next time.

In synthesis

Try to understand your pendings according to their priority: By all means, use a time-management system. But when choosing one, make sure:

- It helps having all pendings listed in *one* place, which is ideally accessible from *any* place (a multi platform app of some kind).
- It prioritizes pendings by *urgency* and *importance*.
- It reflects precedence (via a structure of pendings: Gantts, trees, etc.)

With time, you will get good at this—you will manage your time more efficiently, which will leave more time for you. Use that newfound time wisely. Play with your kids (or share a beer with them if they are adults), visit a friend, have a romantic dinner with your partner, walk the dog in the forest.

If at all possible, do not use the saved-up time to work more. You can save time, but you cannot store it up. Saved time has to be spent wisely and immediately.

PART III

(Where we anticipate the usual setbacks
-and a few new ones- and try
to focus on what's important.)

14

Obstacles and Traps

[Daybreak is near. ROBB STARK (Richard Madden) is the acting lord of Winterfell in the absence of his father, who has been taken prisoner and faces the death penalty in King's Landing, the capital of The Realm. ROBB will march into battle against the powerful army of the illegitimate King Joffrey. His adoptive brother and best friend THEON GREYJOY (Alfie Allen) sits with him in the main room of the fortress]

[THEON] *Are you afraid?*

[ROBB] [EXTENDS HIS TREMBLING HAND] *I must be.*

[THEON] [SMILING] *Good.*

[ROBB] *Good? Why is that good?*

[THEON] *It means you're not stupid.*

(From "Game of Thrones", Season 1, ep. 8 — based on *A Song of Ice and Fire* by George R. R. Martin.)

Up to a point, fear is our friend. Fear plays a crucial role in the survival of any species: It is our instinct telling us about the presence of danger.

There is a catch, though—kind of a "Pascal's wager" situation regarding fear and its relation to danger:

- If we are *not* afraid and there is indeed danger, we are unprepared and vulnerable.

- But if we *are* afraid and there is *no* danger, it was all just a scary moment, nothing else.

For that reason we sometimes learn to react with fear of everything and nothing—"better safe than sorry". But such *preemptive panic* comes with a cost—living afraid takes its toll in terms of health and happiness.

John Strausbaugh expresses it clearly in his book *Sissy Nation*:

> [We] manifested them one by one: conformism, groupthink, consumerism, fundamentalism, political correctness, infantile narcissism, manufactured fears and panics, defeatism, laziness, obesity, gender confusion, the cult of victimhood, the flight from reality into virtuality, the mistaking of a lifestyle for a life, and the confusion of life filled with junk for a fulfilled life.
>
> [...] Now things have sunk to a level where we can finally see they're not separate and discrete problems. They are mutually reinforcing symptoms of one giant Sissy culture that have come together in a perfect storm of Sissitude. We're not just fat, we're not just lazy, we're not just conformists, we're not just narcissists... We're all these things and all the others, rolled up in one big, soft, squishy ball.

And all that has been great for business: self-help books, weapons, Doomsday-prepping TV shows... all thriving, especially after 9/11. We are afraid of everything. Afraid of sickness, of dying, of living, of sex, of food, of the air, the weather, the economy, and a thousand other things.

What do you feel when you look at your new portfolio of activities? If you don't feel even a little fear, then probably your dreams are not big enough. Fear is the indicator of leaving the comfort zone, which is the only way to grow (and, *ergo*, the only way to go).

If you feel *intense* fear instead, it means that your newly designed life might be a tad too ambitious, and it needs revision and adjustment.

Fear is kind of a good friend; just do not let it get *too* close.

Procrastination

Procrastination is *not* a friend. Or at least, procrastination is the way in which *we* become unfriendly to others.

Procrastination can be a symptom of depression. And a generally accepted conclusion is that depression (and consequently procrastination) is repressed anger. If you are procrastinating, maybe you could think what you are so angry about.

Procrastination can be a form of passive-aggression. Physical violence is not the only form that aggression can adopt; passive-aggression is a more subtle form of violence. Not doing things that we (or others) need brings about the consequences associated with that inaction, a sort of punishment, or counterattack.

Procrastination is a paradoxical form of simultaneously fighting and avoiding conflict, and as such it damages us as well. So in a way, it is a form of self-aggression.

Do you see the common denominator in procrastination? *Aggression*. I think that the purpose of procrastination is to attack—other people, ourselves, whomever. I am, of course, not talking about the occasional lazy day (we all have those from time to time) but about a consistent attitude of neglecting significant people, events, and responsibilities.

A deeper discussion on this subject would exceed my qualifications. Let me only say that if you are a chronic procrastinator, you should consider the probable causes listed above. Seeking expert advice would be a useful course of action, too.

Blockages

Classic example: the writer's block. We are writing a book, a thesis, a paper, a report... and suddenly words desert us. It is not laziness: It has to do with an inner, perhaps not-yet-conscious conviction that our work is a fraud, somehow. We are blocked because we *do not believe* in what we are writing.

It happens in all creative, artistic expressions. The distrust is not necessarily related to the quality of our work, but to its propositions. We get blocked when we internally realize that our premises are leading us to untenable conclusions.

Proposed solution: if possible, reconstruct your work on different foundations and premises. If not possible, then it is irreversibly misaligned with your Self, so simply discard it. Beware: you might have to discard much more than just our unfinished drafts; if the problem is in our convictions themselves, they will have to go, too. In time, some new ones will replace them.

Grandiosity and narcissism

Bad news: you are a narcissist. Good news: we all are, and that is okay (up to a point).

Is our narcissism a healthy feature of our psyche, which results in an adequate self-esteem and a healthy exhibitionism, or is it the *pathological* version, instead, which results in an oscillation between arrogance and self-hate?

Negative narcissism is created by the grandiose impulses that pressure the personality from within, generating two kinds of "inflation": a) personal grandiosity; b) idealizing projections that displace the grandiose energies onto other people, institutions, or groups, expressed as religion, race, gender, social class, and so on.

Let's see which one we have.

Signs of a narcissistic personality

- **Hypersensitivity to criticism.** While everyone adores you and compliments your capacities and accomplishments (either real or exaggerated), the *camouflage* of self-esteem remains intact. You start the day feeling like a champion, but after a meeting with your manager in which some things that are not working out as they should are put on the table, suddenly you feel like a failure; a sense of shame and rage invades you, and then extends to other areas of your life: "if I am such a terrible failure at my job, maybe I also suck big time altogether", and suddenly your whole life becomes an excuse for an orgy of self-loathing fueled by an incapacity of excelling *all the time at all things*, as your inflated sense-of-self demands. It's a pretty nightmarish scenario.

- **Unlimited fantasies, behaviors, or claims.** A grandiose sense of *entitlement* that is never satisfied. Unbounded sexual fantasies, whimsical impositions on people around us, acting as victims to obtain special treatment from others—and so we become the abusers ourselves.

- **Underestimating what we are dealing with.** Saying *"I can do this!"* when facing challenges is the good kind of narcissism, like a self-encouragement to stand our ground and face conflicts. The grandiose-narcissistic person, however, *disregards* incoming challenges instead, based on a false sense of superiority. It looks like self-confidence, but it really is a *denial* of conflict. Events usually backfire with such attitude. For example: not prepping enough for a test, interview or meeting; suspending the intake of antibiotics or other medicines as soon as one feels better (*"oh, I am better now, I don't need that anymore"*); becoming sexually promiscuous and putting you and others at risk, etc.

- **Panicking,** which is the opposite, equally extreme reaction to conflict. A mature and balanced personality assigns to each conflict the adequate amount of mental and physical energy; uncontrolled overreaction does not: this is the "just-in-case" type of fear kicking in.

Consequences of narcissism

The key concept behind narcissism is "grandiosity": Our *fantasy-self* writes checks that the "real-us" cannot pay. That either makes us:

- **Manic**; running after any activity that promises to quench those demands (typical of the Da Vinci Cursed); not being able to sleep because your mind is obsessed with all the magnificent books you are going to write or not being able to develop a romantic relationship with one person because you want to possess *every* person that crosses your path. Or addicted, because you want to experience every drop of whatever substance you cannot handle with measure.

- **Depressed**, because at some level we know those desires are so high and unachievable that we soon realize that it is useless to try. Depression is pointed at by notable authors as a *self-regulatory* mechanism that kicks into operation when a grandiose sense of *self* threatens us by making unrealistic evaluations of our situation, possibilities, and rhythms.

There are many roles in society in which a narcissistic personality can perform well. However, such achievements pose an off-the-chart pressure on the person's life, a pressure to overachieve constantly, avoiding at all costs the setbacks that menace an ego excessively vulnerable to failure.

For the Da Vinci Cursed, finding an activity about which we can say: "This is not what I *do*, this is what I *am*" is already difficult. But if, on top of that, our self-perception is distorted by narcissism, our search of that activity is bound to fail.

The following are some examples of how that might happen. Success, failure, pride... they all are relative notions, not absolute ones. They emerge and acquire meaning only after a particular process: **comparison.**

Comparison, a circular argument

The 9.45 train is not the 10.00 o'clock train, even if it runs 15 minutes late. It is not, because it is *precisely* the 9.45, and not some other train.

We understand the world as a system of differences. "To compare" means "to establish a difference", and is therefore essential to our understanding of the world. But not all comparisons are made correctly, and we must be especially careful when *we* are the ones being compared.

A correct comparison takes attributes *one by one*, and measures their values in two or more entities. For example, the following assertions are true for *me* personally:

1. Stephen Hawking is far more intelligent than I am.
2. Harrison Ford has more money and fame than I can ever dream to have.
3. No matter how hard I try, I will never play soccer better than Lionel Messi.

I could go on and on. But consider these comparisons:

1. Harrison Ford and Messi suck at physics.
2. Hawking and Messi suck at acting.
3. Harrison Ford and Hawking suck at soccer.
4. I play better tennis than *any* of them.

Comparison is a *selective* process. Depending on what entities and attributes I take, I can make a favorable comparison or an unfavorable one. "If you compare yourself with others, you may become vain or bitter, for there always will be greater or lesser persons than yourself" wrote **Max Ehrmann** in his famous *Desiderata*. Let's not compare circularly, but *objectively*. A comparison should tell us where we stand regarding the whole spectrum of a particular ability, and (optimally) be indicative of the steps we should take to increase proficiency.

An interesting exercise is to think how Messi, Hawking, or whomever we admire would have resolved a challenge we face right now in our own activity. Comparisons should inspire us to improve, not shame us.

And I suspect that the only *real, useful* comparison is between us, and us-in-an-alternate-universe. How does our actual, current life compare to what it could have been, had we taken a different path? Or better yet: How does "five-years-from-now-Me (if I keep doing the same)" compare with "five-years-from-now-Me (if I dare to follow a different path)"?

It is still a thought experiment, of course. The future "Me's" are only hypothetical. But they are at least *potentially* true—that is, more relevant for a personal comparison than some Hollywood actor or a sports superstar. I am sure they all have their own fair share of skeletons hidden in the closet, anyway.

Shame: its cause and meaning

Feelings of shame and ridicule are not unusual among people with an inflated narcissism: Shame is the sign of a narcissism begging to be kept in check.

I do not refer here to shame in the "social-preventive" sense of the word, where it operates as a warning against unacceptable drives: it helps us function adequately in diverse social situations. Instead, I refer to shame as a sense of inadequacy, humiliation, embarrassment, mortification and despair, generated by the non-achievement of *unrealistic* goals. The failure is real (our goals were not attained), but the real problem is the *goals*. And the situation is worst when we have previously announced our intentions to the world (discussed below).

Shame can be understood as a blow to our sense of self-esteem. The question is: *do we deserve that blow?*

The concept of self-esteem is at the core of most self-help literature. The fundamental problem I see is that they use *more* narcissism to fuel self-esteem increases. Narcissism imposes distorted expectations; failure ensues—our self-esteem suffers, shame begins. So, we artificially try to mend our self-esteem by telling ourselves how valuable ("unique, special, deserving") we are—which is nothing more than the classic narcissistic feeling of entitlement. Doing so redefines expectations in (again) a distorted way, not according to reality but according to how fantastic we supposedly are or must be. The new, unavoidable blow to our self-esteem is logically bigger, one that will (again) need some huge pseudo-self-motivation to be compensated.

It is a vicious circle. Not surprisingly, research shows that those with "high self-esteem" are more vulnerable to the consequences of failures and setbacks because of the devastating effect negative outcomes can have on their self-image.

The Fermat trap

French lawyer **Pierre de Fermat** (1601-1665) was also a brilliant mathematician. Talk about a narcissist: he loved to tease his colleagues challenging them to find the proofs for difficult theorems—proofs he himself claimed to have found, so avoiding peer review while gaining popularity. The biggest tease of his career was a note in a margin of his copy of the *Diophantus' Arithmetica*, in which he wrote, in reference to a conjecture referred to in the book: *"I have found a truly marvelous proof of this proposition, but this margin is too narrow to contain it"*.

For more than three hundred years both amateur and professional mathematicians have tried to produce such a proof, an accomplishment that would immediately catapult the finder to universal fame and recognition. Through the centuries many academies of science have offered monetary prizes to the person who could provide a satisfactory proof. The last contest (sponsored by the University of Göttingen, Germany) was announced in 1908, and it stayed open for 100 years.

Many have found the challenge stimulating and fruitful; a way to improve their knowledge in the process. Others have lost uncountable hours in vain, others yet have lost their minds. The fundamental difference between them lies in the *reason* behind the hunt.

F. R. Schlichting, the mathematician who reviewed the contest entries during the 1970s, wrote to his university's committee:

> Nearly all "solutions" are written on a very elemental level (using the notions of high school mathematics and perhaps some undigested papers in number theory). **The senders are often persons with a technical education but a failed career who try to find success with a proof of the Fermat problem.**[11]

Other versions of the *Fermat trap* are "get-rich-quick" schemes, "get your diploma in 6 months" shortcuts, and "lose 50 lbs. in 3 weeks" scams.

In short: Do not try to get back in the game with one swing. Success demands effort. Don't be "too cool for school": do your homework, pay your dues to your art, science, hobby, profession, or whatever activity incarnates your mission. Commit to a genuine growth. Pledge right now that you will pay the dues that true mastery demands.

Everyone is learning, and everyone is teaching. Even if it is in an informal way (unconscious, virtual, intuitive, etc.), we are all immersed in some kind of *"master-apprentice"* dynamic. Sometimes we are the master, sometimes we are the apprentice. Da Vinci wasn't born ready to paint the Mona Lisa: he washed brushes and swept floors for years at the workshop of his master, Andrea del Verrocchio, where he learned to add direction and rigor to his talents.

Loosening the grip of our narcissism

Our "normal" grandiosity can be confronted by cultivating some concrete attitudes:

- **Create *real* relationships with *real* people.**[12] Your Facebook "friends" do not count. Your family, romantic partners, and real-world friends do.

11: Simon Singh (2005), "Fermat's Last Theorem" - Harper Perennial (emphasys added by me).
12: Moore (2003) - P. 149

- **Stop bitchin' about everything.** When something doesn't turn out as you wanted, swallow it and build character on that disappointment. Don't take everything personally. Do not make a scene, especially regarding "first-world problems" (more about those below).

- **Stop trying to be perfect** and learn the worth of "satisfying", an acceptable balance between costs and benefits. Focus on the important details, not on insignificant minutiae.

- **Avoid self-righteousness.** Self-righteous people are just like know-it-alls: *not welcome*. Stop pushing things down other people's throats and respect their decisions. There are good and bad points of view, but each individual has the right to hold the opinions, tastes, and beliefs he / she pleases—even some despicable ones. You cannot control what's inside other people's heads.

- **Accept failure as a normal part of life.** Nobody wants to fail, but I am tired of that pop psychology that presses us into "never taking a 'no' for an answer", being "winners" all the time, and "never accepting failure, under any circumstance". Sometimes we win, and sometimes we don't: those times we learn. If you never loose, it means you are playing on a level that's too low for you.

Cold, hard cash virtue

The only basis for a *true* self-esteem is **virtue**. Cold, hard cash virtue. Self-esteem is not *per se* a value to maximize: it is a value to *earn*.

How do you know if your self-esteem is genuine or "self-help-books-induced"? Simple. A person with an adequate self-esteem is:

- Not easy to control, or to emotionally hurt with words. The opinion of other people about her is relative.

- Assertive; she will put back in his place anyone behaving with disrespect towards her, and she will do it firmly and serenely. On the contrary, a person with an "artificial" self-esteem may react much more emotionally, a sign that the other person's words have indeed hit a nerve.

To account for self-esteem, enumerating traits is of no use. *"I am intelligent"*. *"I am cute"*. *"I am this or that"*. Who cares? Many of those things are consequences of random, genetic, or otherwise "external" reasons. Particularly useless is *"I am a unique person"*. Yes, but then we all are, so we are "unique" the same.

Cold, hard cash virtue. *What did I do to have the gratitude of another human being? How do I help the world become a better place?* Such are the questions that will direct us to a genuinely deserved self-esteem. Words won't do (as discussed back in chapter 3) —only actions will.

By the way: Fermat's "last theorem" was finally proved in 1997 (358 years after Fermat's marginal note) by Princeton University professor **Andrew Wiles.** He did so in 130 pages of some of the most dense and inscrutable mathematics ever. It took him 11 years of secluded and exhausting work and study, refining existing techniques and developing many new ones.

Specialists, remember? They pay their dues.

15

A Small Catalog of Overrated Things

Mrs. BEVERLY CLARK (Susan Sarandon) meets in a bar with MR. DEVINE (Richard Jenkins), a private investigator she hired to find out more about her husband's lately absences.]

[MRS. CLARK] *Why is it, do you think, that people get married?*

[MR. DEVINE] *Passion.*

[MRS. CLARK] *No.*

[MR. DEVINE] *That's interesting, because I would've taken you for a romantic. Why, then?*

[MRS. CLARK] *Because we need a witness to our lives. There's a billion people on the planet. What does anyone's life really mean? But in a marriage, you're promising to care about everything, everyday. You're saying: "Your life will not go unnoticed, because I will notice it. Your life will not go unwitnessed, because I will be your witness."* [MOVED] *You can quote me on that, if you like.*

Anyway, the reason that I called you here today is to tell you in person that I won't need your services anymore. I think that to continue would be an unwarranted invasion of my husband's privacy and... it's time to stop. Thank you for everything and... goodbye.

[THEY SHAKE HANDS IN SILENCE. THEN HE SAYS]

[MR. DEVINE] *Mrs. Clark, I was right: you are a romantic.*

(From "Shall we Dance", directed by Peter Chelsom, 2004.)

Being a witness. What a concept.

Allow me to get a little too existentialist here.

Yes, the universe is a big, cold place. One is almost *nowhere*. Plus, sooner or later, time erases every trace of *everything* that happened. Almost all deeds go on without notice at all. In such immensity made out of absences and solitude, how do we assign value to things?

Exchanging money for them is a way to recognize value. Granting *time* is a yet more fundamental way of recognition. And I believe that the most important way to recognize the value of things and people is by being *witnesses* to them.

Whatever we grant our attention to receives from us a currency of sorts: the valuable status of not going unnoticed. Conversely, whatever or whomever we ignore gets closer to oblivion (we "don't have time", we are "waiting for the right moment", we "will make it up soon").

Are we being witnesses of the right things?

I think we are not. How could we be, when everything competes for our attention? Advertising is ubiquitous, even in ways we don't notice: politicians and their proselytizing claims; celebrities and their last "secret, 'leaked' sex tape"; religions and their otherworldly claims; TV shows fighting for audience ratings.

The topics we reviewed in this book form a path. In the last chapters:

- We identified and better understood our "curse".
- We recognized the world as a specialized jungle.
- We started to be more attentive to our dark side.
- We started thinking about giving a meaning to our lives, instead of demanding one from it.
- We searched for a specialized, complex and stimulating mission.
- We started to confront our fears and narcissism.

Now all that's left is to follow that path in the real world.

For us DVC's (so easily tempted by everything that shows up at the sides of the road) follow such path means that we have to invest energy in staying focused. We must unmercifully select what are we witnesses of, and ignore overrated, irrelevant, and distracting things. For us, these distractions are like the mythological sirens, whose enchanting songs seduced the sailors onto crashing reefs. Ulysses was clever: he had himself chained to the mast and ordered his crew to put wax in their ears: that way, he would be able to hear the Sirens without being tricked into disaster.[13]

Because of that, dear da Vinci cursed fellow, I present you with this small catalog of overrated and distracting things—reefs in disguise, sirens seducing us as we sail by.

Arguing is distracting

There are some absolute truths. Very few. But they are either indemonstrable or too general to be useful.

The sky is blue; that is true. Except at nights. Except on Mars. Except for the color-blind. Except when it is cloudy. Practical truth (the only usable truth) does not exist: it *consists*.

Once truth is understood as something relative instead of absolute, something interesting happens: **we realize that it is not our job to convince other people of anything.**

It is not our job to shape other people's minds: it's our responsibility to shape our own. So, as soon as an argument stops being necessary, stimulating or cordial, it has to stop. An argument should be a mutual and collaborative evaluation of ideas: as soon as it becomes a penis-measurement contest, excuse oneself and do something else.

Too much explaining is exhausting

I believe we dedicate too much energy explaining ourselves to others. And the worst part is that we set that trap up ourselves. For example:

- **Big announcements.** Each time we announce that we are going to do something (start a new diet, go back to school, whatev-

---

[13]: The Odyssey – Book XII - Attributed to Homer (ca. 850 BC)

er), people hold us accountable later on. *"Hey, weren't you going to start a new diet? What happened? Oh, I see: it was a 'weight gaining' diet, right?"*

- **When we discuss our religious beliefs.** *"So, you are an atheist? Really? And how do you derive your moral rules without a god, then? Why don't you just kill people and rob a bank, if hell doesn't exist anyway?"* Or: *"Christian? Oh, so you believe that a Jewish zombie is watching you 24/7, right?"* For these kinds of "inquiries" perfectly good rebuttals exist, of course. The question is if we should spend any energy giving them to others.

- **When we discuss our political views.** No matter if you are republican, democrat, socialist, libertarian, or whatever, there will be provokers and polemicists tempting you into a discussion. Being a republican or a democrat is fine; being a dialectical sparring partner for others is not.

- **When we discuss especially touchy subjects.** Abortion or the death penalty for example—two subjects with deep social, scientific, moral, and human implications. They are good subjects to discuss from time to time; if possible, with people more intelligent than us and upholders of the opposite position. Or we can just avoid futile discussions altogether and *witness* something else, instead.

- **When we argue with perfect nobodies.** Typical example: Facebook "friends" posting the first stupid thing that comes to their minds. These may be people that you haven't seen for years or some random guy that left a comment on a website (for example YouTube, which is like a magnet for stupid comments). Nonetheless, we feel tempted to jump in the discussion to correct them. Why give them any of our "witness currency" at all?

Susceptibility is immobilizing

A minor lack of courtesy by someone is experienced as an outrageous offense; if someone takes an unfair advantage on us (as in the supermarket checkout lane) we feel sabotaged; when a product or service we bought is not as good as expected we feel defrauded. The slightest insult is taken as a declaration of war. Normal disappointments impact us as intolerable frustrations. We DVC's are particularly sensitive to these "injustices".

Enough. It's time to grow a thicker skin. Let's develop a serene assertiveness. Let's not lose our coolness. Setbacks must be considered business as usual; let's not take everything personally; let's refuse to feel affected by other people's language or behavior.

Many problems are not even problems

Our lives already have (or will have, sooner or later) their fair share of serious problems. Illness, financial struggle, heartbreaks, relationship crises, bereavement, and many others. Those are problems serious enough to require a lot of our physical and mental energy. But others are grossly overrated:

- **"First World problems".** A hair got trapped underneath the protective sheet of your smartphone. The house is a mess, and you can't find the remote. The flight attendant forgot that you ordered a vegetarian meal. You have run out of clean socks, or toilet paper, or cereal. Such problems do not deserve more energy than a silent, subvocalized curse. Then all there is left to do is to solve them or ignore them. Don't let the small stuff drain much of your energy.

- **"Water under the bridge" problems.** Did we screw up something? It's done. Apologize if you can, salvage what you can, learn your lesson, and move on. And if you want, let out a low curse. And that is all there is to it.

- **"Nothing-to-do-about" problems.** It's too cold, or too hot. It's raining, or not. The time goes by too fast, or too slow. The taxes are too high and the next election is years away. You are too tall, or too short. In general: situations that don't depend on you, situations nothing can be done about.

Becoming Ulysses

Let's not live our lives giving a lot of explanations or getting trapped in many arguments. Your real friends don't need them, the stupid will not understand them, your adversaries won't ever be satisfied with them (or will use them against you), and the rest don't care.

Let's reserve clear explanations for the crucial stakeholders of our lives, *our own witnesses*: our spouse, children, and close friends and family—those who need to understand what we are up to so they are not worried about us and who would be happy to be supportive regardless.

Let's spend less time in front of screens, sitting there in zombie-mode watching things other people created. Ads, agitators, celebrities... Let's not be witnesses of that mediocrity. Like the sirens, they all constantly try to lure us into their waters.

Maybe someday we will do not as da Vinci did, but as Ulysses did.

Maybe someday we will tighten the chains we have chosen to wear, staying true to the course we have set to navigate through the turbulent waters of our renaissance spirits. And with firm voice we will order our sails deployed, and we will command to advance toward the horizon, and we will not look back.

Farewell

[BRUCE WAYNE (Christian Bale) is back in Gotham City. To better hide his superhero persona from the world, he acts out the role society expects from a multibillionaire, handsome playboy. He leaves the fancy hotel's restaurant laughing and having fun with two beautiful, soaked blondes —they just bathed in the giant fish tank in nothing but their underwear. As the valet pulls up the Bugatti, they walk past RACHEL DAWES (Katie Holmes)].

RACHEL: *Bruce?* [WAYNE TURNS. RACHEL IS STANDING THERE, DRESSED FOR DINNER, STUNNING]

WAYNE: *Rachel.*

BLONDES: [FROM THE CAR] *Come on, Bruce! We have some more hotels we want you to buy!*

[RACHEL GLANCES AT THEM, THEN BACK AT WAYNE]

RACHEL: *I heard you were back. Where were you?*

WAYNE: *Oh, kind of... all over. You know.*

RACHEL: [SERIOUS] *No, Bruce, I don't know. And neither did a lot of people. People who thought you were probably dead.*

[WAYNE LOOKS AT HER IN SILENCE FOR A MOMENT. THEN HE GESTURES TOWARDS THE BUGATTI AND THE BLONDES AND SAYS:]

WAYNE: *Rachel, all that... —that's not... "me". Inside I'm different. Inside I'm... more.*

RACHEL: *Bruce, it's not who you are underneath, but what you do that defines you.*

(From "Batman Begins", directed by Christopher Nolan, 2005.)

L**et's start anew.**

Our childhood fantasies. Our parents' expectations. Any modest sense of accomplishment we might feel when looking at our *résumés*. The decisions made by the 17-year-old we used to be. The well-meaning advice from other people. Let's leave all that behind.

Via. Weg damit. Adiós. Bye.

Let's drop old expectations and create new ones. Let's forget who we were supposed to be, and let's become who we truly are.

Let's start anew; responsibly, but unstoppably.

Allow me to finish this book borrowing from Thoreau:

> I learned this, at least, by my experiment: that if one advances confidently in the direction of his dreams, and endeavors to live the life which he has imagined, he will meet with a success unimagined in common hours.

Let's advance in the direction of our dreams. If not, what else is left?

After all, it's what we *do* that defines us.

Bibliography

Berlin, 1953: *Isaiah Berlin, The Hedgehog and the Fox: An Essay on Tolstoy's View of History* - Ivan R. Dee, Publisher - 1953

Cottingham, 2003: *On The Meaning of Life* — John Cottingham - Rutledge's "Thinking in action" series, 2003.

Frankl, 1959: *Man's Search for Meaning* — Viktor E. Frankl — Simon & Schuster, 1959.

Goldstein, 1939: *The Organism* — K. Goldstein - New York: American Book Co., 1939.

Hollis, 1994: James Hollis - *Under Saturn's Shadow* — *The Wounding and Healing of Men* — Inner City Books.

Hollis, 2001: *Creating a Life* — *Finding your individual path* — James Hollis — Inner City Books.

Hollis, 2003: *The Middle Passage* — *From Misery to Meaning in Midlife* — James Hollis — Inner City Books.

Jung, 1955: *Mysterium Coniuctionis* — Jung, Carl G. - The Collected Works - Volume 14.

Jung, 1977: *The Symbolic Life: Miscellaneous Writings* - Jung, Carl G. - The Collected Works - Volume 18 - Rutledge and Kegan Paul, Ltd. — Published by the heirs of C. G. Jung.

Jung, 1938: *Psychology and Religion* — Jung, C. G. - The Collected Works11: Psychology and Religion: West and East.

Lore, 2008: *Now What?: The Young Person's Guide to Choosing the Perfect Career* - Nicholas Lore — Touchstone, 2008.

Maslow, 1943: A. H. Maslow — *A Theory of Human Motivation* - Originally Published in Psychological Review, 50, 370-396.

Moore, 2003: Robert Moore, *Facing the Dragon* — *Confronting Personal and Spiritual Grandiosity*. Chiron Publications, 2003.

Morrison, 1989: *Shame* — *The underside of Narcissism*. The Analytic Press.

Niven, 2005: David Niven — *The 100 Simple Secrets of Successful People* — Capstone Publishing Ltd., London.

Segal, 1998: Robert A. Segal (Ed.): *The Myth and Ritual Theory* — *An Anthology* - Malden, Mass. [u.a.] Blackwell, 1998.

Zweig/Abrams, 1991: *Meeting the Shadow* — *The Hidden Power of the Dark Side of Human Nature* — Edited by Connie Zweig and Jeremiah Abrams — Jeremy P. Tarcher/Penguin.

(Notes)

(Notes)

(Notes)

(Notes)

(Notes)

Made in the USA
San Bernardino, CA
30 November 2018